ITIL® and Organizational Change

ITIL® and Organizational Change

PAMELA ERSKINE

IT Governance Publishing

Every possible effort has been made to ensure that the information contained in this book is accurate at the time of going to press, and the publisher and the author cannot accept responsibility for any errors or omissions, however caused. Any opinions expressed in this book are those of the author, not the publisher. Websites identified are for reference only, not endorsement, and any website visits are at the reader's own risk. No responsibility for loss or damage occasioned to any person acting, or refraining from action, as a result of the material in this publication can be accepted by the publisher or the author.

ITIL® is a Registered Trade Mark of the Cabinet Office.

IT Infrastructure Library® is a Registered Trade Mark of the Cabinet Office.

Apart from any fair dealing for the purposes of research or private study, or criticism or review, as permitted under the Copyright, Designs and Patents Act 1988, this publication may only be reproduced, stored or transmitted, in any form, or by any means, with the prior permission in writing of the publisher or, in the case of reprographic reproduction, in accordance with the terms of licences issued by the Copyright Licensing Agency. Enquiries concerning reproduction outside those terms should be sent to the publisher at the following address:

IT Governance Publishing
IT Governance Limited
Unit 3, Clive Court
Bartholomew's Walk
Cambridgeshire Business Park
Ely
Cambridgeshire
CB7 4EA
United Kingdom
www.itgovernance.co.uk

© Pamela Erskine 2013

The author has asserted the rights of the author under the Copyright, Designs and Patents Act, 1988, to be identified as the author of this work.

First published in the United Kingdom in 2013
by IT Governance Publishing.

ISBN 978-1-84928-422-6

PREFACE

Whether your IT organization is embarking on a full-blown IT Infrastructure Library® (ITIL®) process implementation, or you are simply changing existing IT processes, some level of organizational change is required to realize the full benefits. Organizational change is difficult and often slow to occur. Many process- and technology-related initiatives never realize the benefits of their investment as attitudes and behaviors within the organization affect the outcome and, therefore, the benefits are minimized, or, in some cases, non-existent.

ITIL® *and Organizational Change* provides a concise overview of five organizational change models that can help to guide planning for the changes that need to occur in your organization to be successful. Additional guidance is provided relating to key skills, concentration areas, and planning in order to:

- minimize resistance to change related to your ITIL process initiative
- provide a methodology to engage those affected by the changes in the planning and implementation process
- form the governance and project structure to improve project outcomes.

The guidance provided can be applied to almost any initiative, although this book focuses on providing clear, practical advice to help you achieve the return on investment expected from your IT Service Management (ITSM) project, by providing you with the tools to plan and manage organizational change and ensure success.

ABOUT THE AUTHOR

Pam Erskine has over 15 years of leadership experience with a focus on IT and service transformation through clear vision and strategy, process improvement, knowledge management, training, and accountability. In her role, she is accountable for providing best practices, thought leadership, and guidance relating to the ITIL framework.

Pam is a proven leader, having operational responsibility for several IT transformation initiatives with measurable results in customer satisfaction, efficiency, and effectiveness. She has managed staff of 200+ that are focused on providing reliable IT services which are aligned with business needs.

In addition to operational responsibility, Pam has provided consultancy to Fortune 50 companies on IT strategy, IT service management, and organizational change initiatives.

Pam has developed an Advanced Organizational Performance Techniques™ program, entitled AdOPT™, which includes assessments, practices, techniques, and training relating to planning and managing organizational change. Although often applied to the implementation of ITIL best practices, this modular program works well with any initiative requiring a significant shift in organizational behaviors.

Pam is an ITIL Expert, an ITIL Service Manager, is Six Sigma certified, and is a Certified Help Desk Director.

ACKNOWLEDGEMENTS

Over the years, I've worked in many different industries with some great people. I've learned a lot along the way. I was usually hired when significant change was occurring or it was needed.

Working as a part of my team meant that some sort of change was always underway, or you were supporting a major change in some manner. We planned for change using the techniques noted in this book. It was never easy, but it was rewarding. To my team members, who thrived in this environment, thank you. We all grounded each other and when I was having a tough day, you often made me smile by pushing forward to continue the work that was underway.

I had two leaders along the way who really made a difference in my career. Gwen Geier made sure that I always considered every possible outcome when working with team members. While at times I was frustrated, Gwen taught me early in my career how to manage risk while taking care of every member of my team. Bob Weir had high expectations, but he gave me a tremendous amount of freedom to determine how to achieve the right result. He was also there when I needed support and stood beside me during periods of turbulence. Thanks to you both for all of your help and support.

I would like to thank the reviewers of this book for their useful contributions: Dave Jones, Pink Elephant; Geoff Harmer, Maat Consulting; H.L. (Maarten) Souw RE, Enterprise Risk and QA Manager, UWV; and Dave Backham, @TheITILv3Expert.

Acknowledgements

Finally, to my husband Aaron, who has been a sounding board over the years, thanks for listening to the many stories and challenges which come with any transformation initiative. I appreciate all of the love and support you have provided.

CONTENTS

Contents

INTRODUCTION

"It is not necessary to change. Survival is not mandatory"

W. Edwards Deming

Why do some organizations fail to realize the benefits of the Information Technology Infrastructure Library (ITIL) after implementation?

Implementation of the IT Infrastructure Library or ITIL principles and processes can be transformational to the IT organization and, ultimately, the business, however, it is common for organizations to apply the ITIL best practices, yet never realize the benefits of the implementation.

ITIL is a best practice framework. It enables IT Service Management (ITSM). The ITIL framework is meant to be customized based on the organization. When implemented effectively, the positive results can be dramatic with the overall business benefiting, as they have the right technology at the right time to complete their required business objectives. IT organizations will find that the traditional IT silos are significantly diminished; accountability is reinforced; and the implementation and optimization of processes, services, and systems allows the IT staff to spend additional time on the tasks which benefit the organization the most.

While the implementation of ITIL principles and processes is a significant task, many ITIL-related initiatives fail to address the organizational change-related aspects of undertaking such an initiative.

If some of the strategy, processes, and functions associated with ITIL have been implemented, but the organization has not seen a shift relating to service or cost, what went wrong? It is possible that costs are increasing. Perhaps there was investment in an IT service management tool and the processes implemented or changed seem to be inefficient. Leadership and the project manager are wondering what went wrong with the implementation. Maybe, nothing appeared wrong with the implementation, but the team just doesn't seem to be following the process or using the tool.

If the organization isn't realizing the benefits of ITIL, or if costs are rising, or the service appears to be getting worse, it is time to ask how the organizational change addressed the culture of the organization and whether the necessary shift in behavior occurred to support the required end result.

CHAPTER 1: HOW WAS ORGANIZATIONAL CHANGE ADDRESSED DURING THE PROJECT?

Depending on the size of the ITIL-related initiative, a change in attitude and behavior was probably required. Organizational change, which includes behaviors and attitudes, as well as culture, is often a very slow process, but it can be achieved through effective organizational change management. It can take planning and a lot of patience.

Shifts in behaviors and attitudes are difficult at best. Within an organization, there are shared values and beliefs. When large groups of people apply the same value or belief system to an organization, all areas of an organization are affected. New staff joining the organization quickly adapt to the existing system of norms.

Individuals who do not conform are sometimes seen as "difficult." They may even be reprimanded for their inability to get along with others. At times, they may have trouble accomplishing tasks and, therefore, they do not feel successful or valued.

It is extremely stressful to be the lone voice within an organization indicating that a change is needed. Often, management inadvertently discourages this type of behavior by assigning issue resolution to whoever brings a problem to light, or by failing to acknowledge the individual voicing the concern.

Individuals within the organization also have their own goals and objectives. Perhaps they want to advance, retire, transfer, or find another job. The belief system of the organization may affect how an individual's goals and objectives are displayed and, therefore, managed within an organization. Does the organization recognize and value advancement? Do they have a history of long-term employees?

In addition, there are sub-cultures within an organization; the sub-cultures may be age or ethnicity based, or related to the length of employment, or perhaps based on some other factor.

Given that the organization shares the same belief system and new team members quickly adapt to the challenges that may exist within the management structure when dealing with change, you can see why it is a challenge to shift the culture of any organization. For organizational change to result in a true cultural shift planning is required and shouldn't be taken lightly. It requires planning, precise execution, and, most importantly, communication with those directly impacted, their direct leaders, and even executives within the organization.

It is important to note that people don't push back merely because change is occurring. They push back when they feel threatened. New or changed processes, reporting, and system changes can pose a potential threat. They may no longer be an expert when completing their work. There may be a feeling that a different standard is emerging and they are not prepared to meet the objectives, as they have not been engaged or trained in the new way of completing the work. Throughout this book, there is an emphasis on communication with those affected by change. To take it a step further, engagement is required. People experiencing change are less likely to be intimidated if they have a voice in the process and they can understand and anticipate how the change may impact their ability to complete their work successfully and contribute to the overall success of the initiative.

Has the organizational change required for success been defined and addressed within the IT service management project?

If the cultural aspects of change were not addressed, or if the change was not sufficiently addressed based on the complexity and true scope of what was expected within the organization, perhaps this is why the benefits of the recent ITIL-related changes are not being realized.

Leaders within an organization often say that team members need to support and follow the direction that is provided. To some degree, this is true, however, it is not realistic. If those affected by the change don't believe in the change that is occurring, if they don't feel as though their voice is heard, or don't see the benefit to the organization and to themselves, what happens?

In the scenarios noted above, some individuals will change their behavior and conform, however, more than likely, while there may be some changes, there will be areas that are lacking, or changes that never fully take place as true buy-in does not exist. Team members may fail to provide valuable feedback which could greatly benefit the implementation, as they don't believe in the change occurring. Passive-aggressive behavior may also come to light. Examples of passive-aggressive behavior include: "forgetfulness" relating to assignments which ultimately negatively affect the project or the service being delivered; poor performance as the individual is not happy with the changes to the process and procedures; moodiness as the individual completes their work, but ensures everyone around them knows they are not happy; and failure to support their colleagues by withholding specific information, thereby causing their co-worker to fail at their tasks.

Do the behaviors noted sound familiar? Does it relate to the ITIL process implementation? Perhaps you have witnessed similar behavior with other projects. Everything described above relates back to organizational change. In the upcoming chapters, we'll explore some organizational change models and methods that can assist with managing some of these issues in order to recognize the benefits of an ITIL process implementation.

Project selection

In order to recognize how the ITIL process implementation is affected by the culture of the organization, let's explore why the initiative was given enough importance to proceed to implementation.

Hopefully, there is an understanding of why the organization made the choice to implement ITIL: the value to the overall organization as it relates to improving service, reducing costs, and meeting the needs of the business. If there is a gap relating to understanding the underlying factors associated with the company creating the ITIL or broader ITSM project, the first step in the journey to tackling the organizational change issue should be interviewing key individuals within the company to understand why they undertook this project. The interview process should involve the decision maker and key executives who were part of the initial conversation.

If these individuals are no longer with the company, or they have transitioned to another role, take some time to identify the key stakeholders in the implementation. Who has the most to gain? Which team will experience the most dramatic changes in how they operate? The answers to these questions should help to identify the right people to engage in the interviews.

Often executives are happy to discuss the drivers for the ITIL implementation once they understand why the question is being asked, so prepare an introduction which explains why this is important, and a short series of questions. Some potential questions are noted below.

- What was the driving factor for the ITIL implementation?
- What is the value of ITIL to the business?
- What is your view on the value to IT?
- What outcomes would you like to see as a result of the implementation?
- How would the outcomes be measured?

Understanding why the ITIL initiative was deemed important enough to implement within the organization will help to frame communications with key stakeholders; establish sound goals; create meaningful metrics; and develop the organizational change plan. Merely having the conversation with key stakeholders or executives will begin the process of promoting the change required. Discussion at the senior level is important to ensure buy-in with leadership and further solidify the goals and objectives of the project.

1: How was Organizational Change Addressed during the Project?

The value proposition

After understanding why the ITIL initiative was selected for implementation, exploration of how the various areas are impacted, as well as the value proposition for each area and/or generic position should be investigated.

The value proposition for IT should also be considered and documented for future use in conversations and various communications. What are the benefits to IT arising from an ITIL implementation? Some examples of benefits are noted below.

- Repeatable processes resulting in consistent service.
- Minimized down time and business disruption, as changes to the IT environment are budgeted, planned, and managed.
- An understanding of the objectives and outcomes of the business.
- An assurance that work takes place on the right activities to meet the business needs.
- Lower costs with improved return on investment.
- Improved relationships with the business.
- Meaningful metrics.

What is the value proposition for IT teams?

- Less time is wasted as work is done on the right projects.
- Repeatable processes result in fewer reactionary events, such as system down time.
- Relationships are improved between IT teams as expectations are defined.
- Metrics allow teams to know how they are doing
- Relationships are improved within the business as expectations are known.

1: How was Organizational Change Addressed during the Project?

What is the value proposition to the IT staff member?

- Responsibilities are succinctly defined allowing the individual staff member to build expertise in their assigned area.
- Relationships are improved within IT; handoffs between teams are easier.
- Meaningful metrics allow team members to know how their team is doing and the metrics are used to improve the process.
- Interactions with the business are less stressful as expectations are known.
- Information is available to support the technology.
- Information is available to understand the known issues and business needs and, therefore, the technology is improved.
- IT completes the right activities and projects, so there is less wasted time.

What about the benefits to the business? Ultimately, IT needs to provide the business with the technology and services necessary to meet their objectives and achieve the required outcomes. IT should effectively support the business. It is why IT exists within the organization.

How does the ITIL project affect the business? ITIL and ITSM affect the business by enabling IT to:

- provide value by strategic partnering/consulting
- engage at the planning and budgeting cycles
- understand business objectives
- manage the service portfolio based on the needs of the business
- invest in the right technology to meet the business need

- provide some transparency in the cost of services, thereby enabling decisions based on cost, risk, and quality which will lead to less waste of both funding and human capital
- retire services/technology when appropriate
- provide the right level of service to meet the business need
- provide the right types of services and technology
- provide the right hours/levels of service
- prioritize services
- provide access points, such as a catalog, service desk, e-mail, chat, field service, and/or walk-up center.

There are intangible benefits to the ITIL implementation as well. Improved relationships with the business and between IT organizations are often a result of improved, measurable processes.

CHAPTER 2: ORGANIZATIONAL CHANGE

The human aspects of change

If the present state of condition shifts to a new state – change has just occurred. ITIL-related implementations can represent a major shift in how work is done. The extent of the change varies from company to company.

What motivates people to change?

There are numerous books on employee motivation. The changes that need to occur within the organization affect employees at all levels. Change scares most people. Unbelievably, change scares people at all levels. Most likely, they won't admit it. They don't even realize that they are afraid to make a change.

Why does change affect them in this manner?

When a change occurs, learning needs to take place. We need to learn about the new process or procedure. What happens if we make a mistake? Will the change result in job loss? What if the change means that we are ineffective in our role? It really is self-doubt. A small percentage of individuals may become so overwhelmed by self-doubt that they self-select. They feel they cannot succeed and they will opt out. It is important that we recognize this potential outcome and accept it.

Of course, the goal is for everyone to succeed. Extra steps are often taken to help those experiencing difficulty, but at some point, it is critical to the morale of the team and the success of the change that steps are taken to correct unresolved employee-related issues. The inability to complete a task appropriately is usually fairly easy to resolve through additional training and holding the team accountable. The negative attitude that an employee sometimes displays is more challenging, however, it cannot be ignored, as this issue can be even more detrimental to the entire team than someone who is having difficulty completing the revised process appropriately. A negative attitude is often a sign of an employee who is uncomfortable with the change itself and their abilities to perform at the same level given the changed environment.

How do we address the self-doubt?

It is important to provide people with information about the ITIL project and the changes that will occur. Perhaps a routine weekly e-mail, newsletter, lunch and learn session, or some other kind of communication.

Training and documentation relating to the change is also imperative to success. Every individual needs to feel that they have the tools and knowledge necessary to do their job. While the change may seem minor to us, to the individual responsible for the end result, it may be overwhelming. Their leaders should be prepared to help them achieve success, but we should also ensure there are additional communications coming directly from the project, or from the person who is responsible for the change. It is always good to provide people with multiple options for obtaining information and asking questions.

When a mistake is made during the transitionary period, it should be a safe environment that reinforces an appreciation for trying to make a shift in the process. We should celebrate their coming forward and asking how to address the problem correctly. In addition to considering if changes are needed to the process, consideration should be given to how we can announce the mistake and send a positive reinforcing message to everyone that it is okay to make a mistake. Ask the individual experiencing difficulty if there is anything that should be considered in terms of changing the process. It is a great learning opportunity for the project and leaders within the organization.

If there is evidence of success with the new process, or the larger IT service management initiative, it is critical to publicize the success. Although some benefits are intangible, use metrics when possible. Start by recognizing individual successes, as well as department successes. While it is great to have a project manager or ITIL process team member recognize the success, engage senior leaders in the recognition process. Sincere recognition from senior leaders often goes a long way toward motivating employees to take ownership of the end result. In addition, quite often, senior leaders are accountable for employee engagement related numbers. Employee engagement refers to an employee's commitment, involvement, and satisfaction in their work. If employees have an emotional and intellectual commitment to their work and the associated mission and vision, their performance is positively impacted resulting in better outcomes. A sense of ownership will exist which often leads to improved service and, overall, a better end result for both the company and the customer.

Senior leaders often fail to recognize just how much their actions and words can impact the success of an initiative or team. Visible support for the implementation of ITIL practices and processes is a step in the right direction. In *Chapters 6* and *7*, we'll talk about the importance of communication and the various change-related roles that are significant to the implementation. Senior leadership will be core to the success of organizational change. Routine public appreciation and recognition from this level of management will often significantly influence employee engagement scores and can have a positive effect on an employee's motivation to implement and succeed at the changes requested.

The Human Resources (HR) team in most companies can offer assistance and guidance relating to organizational development, employee development, various employment-related regulations and issues, and enhancing employee performance. If the HR team is available to participate in the planning and implementation of an ITIL initiative, they are often an invaluable resource that can provide significant guidance on planning for the organizational change necessary to be successful.

True stories from the frontline: the human aspect of change

Years ago, I was recruited to work for a company that was having some challenges with their IT department meeting the needs of the customers. The problems were years in the making, but the challenges were vast and new leadership wanted change.

2: Organizational Change

While the new Chief Information Officer (CIO) wanted change, aside from hiring me, he was actually pretty patient with the situation. I, on the other hand, was not.

Every day, I went to work and took call after call from unhappy customers. I quickly grew to dislike picking up my phone. If it wasn't an unhappy customer, it was my boss telling me he just spoke to an unhappy customer.

As I was new to the company, I understood some of the challenges. I went out of my way to use the normal channels to request help and assistance with my IT needs. I contacted the service desk just like everyone else. I had access to the software that was used to manage my requests and incidents and I watched my incident notifications bounce around from department to department with only minimal work taking place. Little work was being done, but there was a lot of finger pointing. The staff didn't know who I was quite yet, so I was treated just like every other customer.

Meanwhile, I visited the various IT departments within the division, I talked with employees and watched their interactions, I looked at job descriptions and productivity reports, and I interviewed customers about what the team did well and where they needed help.

Throughout these analyses and observations, I continued to hear from unhappy customers. Now that I was talking to the customer community, I was forming relationships with customers and was getting even more calls. I'm glad they called as this was another data point to help pinpoint problems, but it was also very stressful; I needed to ensure that their problems were resolved and I spent my days apologizing for a mess that I didn't create. Things needed to change, or I had to leave; I didn't want to work in an environment where my entire day would be spent making apologies and reacting to various fires.

After a few weeks, some of the changes that needed to occur were clear. Job descriptions needed to be redefined; expectations outlined; a new department needed to be created; and training needed to occur for the existing team. This was only the beginning, but they were important first steps.

I met with my management team and outlined the vision for fixing the problems. It was going to take time, but with the initial steps, progress would be made. We began working on the job descriptions for the existing staff and defined the new roles as well. From my perspective, if we could take the team to the next level, it would be beneficial to all. Raising their skill sets was going to benefit them as well. They would get certifications and, eventually, their salary ranges would rise.

My management team consisted of staff that were new to the organization. Only one person had any tenure and she really wasn't given management responsibilities prior to my arrival. The management team was excited about the changes. We clearly saw the benefits to the organization and the employees. We enthusiastically put together a presentation for the team about the changes.

All of the job descriptions and organizational changes were approved by HR. We were ready to proceed. We scheduled a meeting with the team for a Friday afternoon. The changes were going to be effective within one week.

We gathered the team together to announce and discuss the changes. We showed them the presentation and explained how their roles would change. We talked about the organizational benefits. We talked about training for them. We reviewed the longer-term vision and gave them a snapshot of additional changes to come.

The more we talked about their new roles and the organization, the quieter the team became and you could feel the tension in the room. It was palpable. At the end of the presentation, we asked if there were questions. The room was silent. We handed out the new job descriptions. We indicated that managers would be meeting with their individual team members to create their training plans. Still the room was quiet, but you could feel the tension and if body language was an indicator, some of the staff were downright angry.

Finally, when we asked once again for questions, someone asked how we determined how the roles would change. We talked about best practices and industry standards. We talked about the challenges that were occurring in the environment and discussed the skill sets required. The staff looked at us as though we were crazy.

While my management team was talking, I sat there wondering why they were visibly upset. This was a good change for them. I had told them that their salary could go up by 30%. What was the problem?

The same person who inquired about the role changes replied to the management team and asked why the team wasn't involved in determining a course of action. There were specific aspects of their roles that were going away and it was upsetting. A dam broke in the room and all of the employees began expressing their frustration with the changes and their roles. Even the new organizational chart appeared to be a source of anger.

We managed through the meeting and then regrouped. The changes needed to occur. We revised some plans, but moved forward. It was not an easy transition by any means. Even with extensive training and cost, the changes didn't entirely have the desired result. We made progress and the customer satisfaction was higher, but we just didn't get to where we needed to be to meet the needs of the community and operate effectively and efficiently.

As most of the management team was new to the organization, there were aspects of the culture that we just didn't realize. A restructuring of this magnitude had never occurred in the history of the company.

Some of these employees had been in their roles for years. While the employees may not have been the most experienced, or the best at what they did, they were comfortable. They had carved out a niche for themselves. We were completely revising their jobs.

The employees didn't know the management team. When we introduced these changes, I had been on board less than three months. I hired most of the managers, so they had even less tenure. The one person with tenure in the organization just didn't have management credibility, as they hadn't functioned in a leadership role. The team had no reason to trust us.

We indicated that the bar was being raised. Yes, we told them that there would be training, but for those that were experts, we were completely shaking up their world. For those that weren't necessarily performing well, they say the writing was on the wall. They were used to freedom and we were implementing accountability and metrics.

I had completely missed the human aspects of change. I didn't plan for it. I didn't engage the staff. I didn't communicate early enough and the team had no reason to trust me.

All of the initial changes that I outlined took place and more. I was incredibly successful in turning around the IT team at this company. It took a Herculean effort on my part and the part of my management team. We also lost some good team members that probably could have been saved.

They say that large job-related changes can cause individuals to go through the five stages of grief similar to experiencing the death of someone close to them. While I have no doubt some of the team went through this cycle, the management team also went through this cycle when they dealt with the issues and the fallout from the changes.

I learned some valuable lessons during this effort. Considering the human aspect of change and appropriately planning for it not only results in a better outcome for the customer, it is much easier on the employees and the changes become much easier to manage.

CHAPTER 3: ORGANIZATIONAL CHANGE MODELS

There are several organizational change models. A quick search of the Internet will show that there is an abundance of information available. In this book, we'll focus on the basics of five models. From the author's perspective, some models complement each other and they can be used in tandem. Each model can easily be applied to an IT service management initiative. Some models focus more on employee-related goals associated with change, while others may focus more on ensuring a 360-degree understanding of the change, or techniques for managing resistance. Based on the overview of the models and the culture of the organization, an appropriate model for the project should be selected.

ADKAR®

The ADKAR® model was created by Prosci in the late 1990s (*www.prosci.com*). It focuses on activities that achieve results. It is a goal-oriented change model. This model can assist with diagnosing resistance to change and setting development-related goals for the individuals involved in the change. There are five key areas associated with this model.

- Awareness of the need to make a change.
- Desire to participate and support the change.
- Knowledge of how to make the change.
- Ability to implement the change.
- Reinforcement to keep the change in place.

The ITIL initiative within the organization was identified as a business need. Why? In *Chapter 1*, we recommended uncovering the drivers behind this initiative and translating these into a value proposition. By understanding the drivers, the first key area of ADKAR can be addressed: **Awareness**. Why is the change necessary?

For the awareness phase, information is gathered about why the changes are necessary. This information provides a solid base for the communications that will be defined in the communication plan. It can also provide some input into additional tasks for the organizational change plan. When reviewing why the changes are necessary, are there any additional tasks that should be added to the plan?

The goal is to create awareness within the organization regarding the change, the motivating factors, the desired end result, the timeline for the changes, and details about who will be working on the project. Most of the work in the awareness phase relates directly to communication. When communicating, include baseline metrics relating to service, if possible, so improvements and challenge areas can be addressed without surprise as the project progresses.

Desire is the second key area associated with the ADKAR change model. Desire is really motivation. What are the positive and negative outcomes for individuals affected by this change? As discussed in *Chapter 2*, people are often scared of change. It is important to note the positive outcomes associated with this change. Refer back to the value proposition in *Chapter 1*, as it may help to identify some positive aspects associated with the ITIL process initiative.

How can an employee be affected negatively? As the initiator of the change, it may be difficult to see the negative aspect. From an employee's perspective, they may feel as though they will no longer be an expert in their process or technology area. Remember, knowledge is often power. People enjoy being sought out for advice and input. Another negative aspect is that they may feel as though there is the potential for them to lose their job, or somehow their importance will be diminished.

When looking at desire, it is important to publicize the positive, but also to be open and honest when confronted with potential negative outcomes. Don't be afraid to say that the outcome is unknown if there is uncertainty. The goal is to create a desire to make the change. When reviewing the organizational change plan, what may be missing to address this phase of change? What will motivate people to make the change?

What does the term **Knowledge** mean? Is it the inherent knowledge of the team to do their jobs? Documentation? Training? Regarding the ITIL initiative, what skills, knowledge, and abilities are required to be successful with the change? Is training required? Have the right people been engaged to understand what is really required?

Earlier in the ADKAR model, it was mentioned that knowledge may be power. Everyone loves the recognition of being an expert in his/her field. Now, the way work is completed is changing. Who is the expert? Right now, the expert in the process is the change initiator, but the real expert in the way work is done today is the person performing the job. The process knowledge needs to reside with the frontline person. There may be a large gap between the way the process is defined and what will actually work in practice. Have the team members responsible for the outcome in the process been engaged in process creation?

If they were engaged and their feedback was incorporated, there may be a very solid process in place and some support for the change probably exists. If they were not engaged, research should be conducted to understand if a gap exists first prior to training them on the process. The staff responsible for the outcome must be appropriately positioned to succeed. A preliminary step in the knowledge area should be a review of the process with those responsible for the work.

The knowledge phase is all about ensuring individuals have what they need to be successful. To understand what is required, two steps should occur. Meetings with leadership to understand what training and behavior changes are necessary to ensure success is a smart first step. In addition, a meeting with all, or a subset of, the individuals who are responsible for doing the job to understand the current state and discuss the changes necessary to meet the overall objectives. If possible, this session should occur without leadership in the room to improve the chance of a candid conversation. The agenda should consist of an overview of the change, the timeline, and the expected outcomes. Include examples of how outcomes will be communicated and talk through any key learning to date. The process for determining what changes need to occur should also be included. Work with the individuals in attendance to determine where gaps in knowledge exist and talk through the best way to rectify the gap. Conducting this session with the individuals responsible for the outcome will help them to invest in the change. It is also a step toward setting expectations.

The tasks to address knowledge should be included in the organizational change plan. There may be tasks associated with updating the job descriptions to include the new requirement. The communication plan may need some tasks to communicate important topics, such as the completion or availability of training and documentation.

The **Ability** phase refers to the ability to implement new skills and behaviors. If steps are taken to provide the awareness, instill desire, and provide the knowledge, is it safe to assume that someone now has the ability to change? This phase is all about turning knowledge into action. Sometimes there can be a significant gap between knowledge and ability. Consideration regarding the ability to change should be evaluated at the individual, team, department, division, and company level.

To ascertain the ability to change at the various levels, evaluation of the individual level is a good place to start. Engaging the individuals who are required to change in a discussion about how they are feeling about the change and their ability will once again provide them with a feeling of inclusion. It also creates an open conversation about any remaining gaps in the process or their knowledge. If there is an opportunity to have some hands-on practice sessions relating to the change, it will increase the confidence level of those involved.

Upon reviewing the individual's ability to change, it is easier to move to the next level of the organization. The team, department, or division level is next on the list. Again, this can be managed by engaging in conversation with the area and their leader.

When meeting with individuals to assess their ability, a simple list of questions regarding the change and their readiness can provide some structure to the conversation.

- Do you feel ready to implement the changed process?

- Was your training sufficient?
- Do you have the documentation you need to perform the process?
- Have you practiced the new procedure?
- Do you feel as though you know how to escalate issues requiring clarification?

Address any potential issues which may negate the ability to perform the change or negatively affect the implementation. Some of the feedback received may relate to resistance to change. It is important to assess what is a true gap in ability versus difficulty with change. By now, there have been numerous conversations with those affected, so the amount of resistance to the change should be diminishing.

Remember, the ability phase is all about turning knowledge into action. Additional tasks relating to process changes, training, documentation, etc. may have been identified for the organizational change, or project plan, during the ability assessment discussions. Has a clear communication path been established to allow those affected to ask questions or escalate issues? It is important that those affected feel as though they have the support they need. There may be some organizational change tasks noted that are associated with how the escalations are handled.

Reinforcement refers to the ability to retain and sustain the change once it has been made. Once a change has occurred, it is normal to move on to the next task, however, consideration should be given to sustaining the changes. Metrics should be used throughout the implementation and the results shared with the group. If the results are not as expected, additional focus groups, or one-to-one interviews should occur to determine how to achieve the desired end result.

It is important to recognize the achievement of those who made the necessary changes. Numerous options are available, such as public verbal recognition, a note of appreciation, project-related celebrations, etc. The important note here is really to celebrate success and reinforce the importance of the work that was completed.

Metrics are part of reinforcement

What does success look like in terms of organizational change for an ITIL implementation, or any process change or implementation? Success will vary dramatically from organization to organization. Each organization is unique in terms of their industry, size, ITIL project, and defined goals and objectives. Success for one organization may be defined as improving customer satisfaction, while another organization may have goals related to streamlining operations in order to reduce headcount. Success for each organization is different, as it is based on their needs and the value proposition of the project.

Without understanding the baseline performance, it may be difficult to know if success has been achieved. Organizational change can be measured in many ways. The change itself supports the IT service management or process specific initiative. The actual metrics associated with the process outcomes are certainly considered success measures for the change itself.

Employee performance measures are also indicators of success. Perhaps the implementation of knowledge management allowed the service desk representative to improve their first contact resolution number, or the implementation of incident management improved customer satisfaction for the infrastructure team.

There are numerous ways to understand success of the organizational change. Division level metrics and employee engagement scores are potential areas to consider. Regardless of the status of the ITIL initiative and the associated organizational change, it is important to identify meaningful metrics. A baseline should be established to understand the starting point and a vision is needed for what constitutes success.

Throughout the project, the progress against baseline metrics should be monitored to determine if adequate forward momentum is occurring. Adjustments should be made as necessary. Finally, at the end of the initiative, it is important to know the end result. As with any initiative, sustainment measures should be determined and implemented as part of a continual cycle of improvement. As noted within the ADKAR materials, reinforcement is ongoing.

Throughout the lifecycle of the project, transparency of metrics within the team, affected departments, and the overall division, is important, both as a reinforcement tool and to help build a culture of process improvement. Remember, the reaction to negative movement in the numbers should be approached with a mindset geared towards correcting the problem, rather than harsh words. Reacting appropriately to both positive and negative momentum will help to build a team that values process improvement and actually suggests ways to improve upon the existing state.

In the reinforcement phase, there will be additional tasks identified for the organizational change and project plans. Communication regarding the metrics and changes resulting from the metrics may result in tasks for the communication plan. Perhaps there are changes to the performance appraisal process to ensure ongoing reinforcement of the change. What tasks should be added to the project plan, organizational change plan, and communication plan to ensure long-term success of the change? Consideration should also be given to continual service improvement relating to the processes being implemented. How will they be refined and modified?

Six Change model

While ADKAR is a model which focuses on activities associated with change and planning for them, the Six Change model focuses on minimizing or decreasing resistance to change. It includes methods for dealing with change resistance which can be used in tandem with ADKAR. The Six Change model was created by Kotter and Schlesinger in the late 1970s.

According to Kotter and Schlesinger (1979), there are four reasons people resist change (*see also* Rance, 2011 and Kotter, 1996).

1. **Self-interest:** The impact on the individual is considered over the positive impact to the organization.
2. **Misunderstanding:** Information about the change is not understood, is unavailable, or is confusing resulting in assumptions.
3. **Low tolerance to change:** The change will disrupt the routine. Perhaps the resident "expert" on a subject will

no longer be the expert. A feeling of insecurity exists with change.

4. **Different assessments of the situation:** Disagreements exist over the change and/or the positive or negative benefits over moving forward.

The Six Change model includes six approaches to deal with resistance to change. All aspects of the model involve significant communication with those affected by the change; engagement with those affected is also stressed.

1. Education and communication

The education and communication step is fairly self-explanatory. As with ADKAR, there is a focus on ensuring that training and education has occurred. In addition, communication often and early is recommended to ensure staff members feel some ownership of the change.

An emphasis is made on talking with the team regarding their needs to be successful. Assessing the changes to the process and ensuring proper training and/or knowledge is available is recognized as being critical to the success of the change. Explain why the ITIL improvements are necessary and communicate the unifying purpose, so those affected can understand how the change and, ultimately, their performance links back to the underlying problem, as well as the overall success of the initiative.

2. Participation and involvement

The participation and involvement step of Six Change is all about engaging those affected, so they feel connected to the changes that are occurring. This relates to engaging staff in the changes that are occurring.

With an ITIL implementation, staff members can sometimes really struggle with feeling that their input regarding the process is valued. ITIL is a series of best practices that is meant to be customized based on the organization. Those impacted by the change are often a part of the existing process. They have a lot of knowledge on what is working and how things can be improved. Engaging them in early conversations and incorporating their feedback where it makes sense can provide them with a feeling of ownership in the change, thereby making acceptance of the change a little easier.

3. Facilitation and support

Those impacted by change need to feel supported. Providing them with escalation paths when they experience difficulty, or when they need assistance, is critical to effective support.

With any new initiative, unanswered questions, or uncertainty regarding the appropriate course of action, may exist at times. Empowering staff to make decisions about how to proceed during periods of ambiguity and, subsequently, supporting their decisions will encourage participation and provide them with a sense of ownership regarding the success of the initiative.

Managers in the organization should be provided with information regarding the change, project plans, and success metrics. They also need to know where to go for information and assistance. Managers often have to deal with the anxiety or resistance to change from their employees, so it is important to have regular conversations with them to ensure they are armed with what they need to successfully support the ITIL initiative.

4. Negotiation and agreement

In negotiation and agreement, the participation of those affected is again stressed, just as in participation and involvement. The negotiation and agreement approach encourages those affected to be given the ability to veto aspects of the change, if there is justifiable concern. When applying this to an ITIL initiative, consider allowing those responsible for process execution to veto a particular aspect of the process, or the associated metrics, provided they can provide an acceptable alternative that ultimately supports the business in meeting their objective, while supporting the overall efficiency and effectiveness of the IT organization. Applying this negotiation method will ultimately result in a better outcome for the organization and the employee will feel a sense of pride with the end result.

The negotiation and agreement phase also encourages leaders to incentivize individuals to be supportive of the change, rather than change resistant. While incentives are always nice, be sure to use them to reward or encourage the right behavior. If an individual is extremely change resistant, be careful to reward a supportive behavior, rather than trying to find some way of giving an incentive even if a behavior doesn't exist.

When managing an employee who is expressing significant concern regarding the change environment, it is normal to feel a sense of relief when they contribute to the change in a supportive way. Be careful not to reward them for displaying supportive behavior after being difficult. It is common for leaders to experience a sense of gratitude when a difficult employee, or employee situation, is minimized. Rewarding an employee for displaying the same positive behavior as others on the team, after a challenging period, can be demeaning to the remainder of the team and it potentially sends the wrong message. Consider praising the difficult employee's input during a private one-to-one conversation.

5. Manipulation and co-option

Manipulation and co-option is exactly what it appears to be. In the case of significant resistance, bring the resistor and possibly their leader into the project as a team member. The thought is to give them a voice in a manner where they cannot do any harm to the outcome. The goal is to turn them into a supporter.

When asking for input, or bringing resistors into the fold, be careful. If there is a perception that they are not being heard, or that they are being manipulated, their behavior may become worse.

While it may be a risk, consider giving the resistor a task of substantial importance. With an ITIL initiative, process development, tool requirements, and identification of metrics are all examples of important tasks which require a substantial amount of work, thereby allowing the resistor to become more familiar with the initiative and to develop a sense of purpose within the project. Work with them one-to-one to ensure they are on the right track and provide them with the support necessary to succeed.

6. Explicit and implicit coercion

The explicit and implicit coercion approach relates to forcing employees into accepting the change by being very clear that change resistance will have a negative result, such as termination, or the lack of an annual salary increase.

While this approach is considered extreme by some, it is a reasonable approach if rapid change is required, or if there is extreme resistance to changing the way work is completed. Using this approach does not negate trying other methods first. Prior to using this approach, be sure that other options have been reviewed and implemented where appropriate.

If explicit and implicit coercion is the course of action, set attainable goals for those affected and ensure that metrics are in place to measure success. Rather than implying that there may be a consequence, be very straightforward. Work with the human resources team to be very explicit and document the requirements for those affected, along with the measure of success.

Freeze Change model

The Freeze Change model was developed by Kurt Lewin (1947). The model is focused on three simple stages. It is based on the idea that the majority of people are in their comfort zone. They are like a block of ice. They need motivation to leave the comfort zone, as change will not occur until people are uncomfortable. For change to occur, the ice must unfreeze, change, and be frozen again.

Stage one involves preparing the organization for change. It is called **Unfreezing**. In this stage, there is significant analysis and communication taking place. Often, the analysis completed determines there is a need to change. In Kurt Lewin's model, he recommends using a force field analysis to weigh the need to change. With a force field analysis, evaluation takes place regarding the driving factors of change and the restraining forces, or the obstacles. If the driving factors outweigh the obstacles, the need for change is justified.

With an ITIL initiative, the driving factors may be: increased customer demands, organizational reliance on technology, competitive advantage, new technology, shrinking funding, etc. The obstacles may be: funding, organizational churn, lack of knowledge, etc. Whatever the factors that drove the ITIL initiative in the organization, they should be shared with the team, so they understand why the change is necessary. In addition, as discussed in *Chapter 1*, the value proposition for each audience should be understood and promoted as part of stage one.

Aside from completing analysis, stage one involves preparing the organization to change. This preparation involves sharing the need for change, the urgency, and the impact on the organization of not changing. Preparing the organization is fundamentally selling them the idea of change. It is an opportunity to build momentum and create awareness regarding the business case for change. It is also the first opportunity to really engage people, so they feel as though they have a voice in what is occurring. Whether they are engaged in the analysis, or perhaps they are given assignments in stage two to determine the changes needed, it is crucial to ensure staff are actively engaged in the ITIL initiative.

As stated in previous chapters, engagement of staff is much more likely to produce a positive outcome, as it allows them to take ownership of the changes that are occurring. Assigning or changing process ownership for the various ITIL processes and forming teams to improve or implement each process is a positive step, as it will help employees to feel connected to the initiative as they are actively participating in the project.

Engagement may also distract the employee from focusing on how their job is changing, as they become more focused on the project and their contribution. Those employees who are not directly engaged in stage one and stage two may focus on what is occurring around them, rather than accomplishing their day-to-day responsibilities. Strong leadership is required in stage one to provide reassurance that the changes are good for the company and the employees.

It can be difficult to unfreeze the organization. As noted earlier, people tend to stay in their comfort zone. It represents safety to them. They know their current role and the organization. They know how to navigate and get things done. If something changes, they will no longer be versed in the process. Lewin's model requires that people move out of their comfort zone. Various techniques can be used to start the transition, examples include:

- Share the analysis regarding why the ITIL implementation, or change, must occur. What are the driving factors? What will occur if the change doesn't happen?
- Set objectives for individuals related to the change, but don't tell them how to accomplish the objective. In this phase, the need is merely to move them out of their comfort zone. The objectives should be related to IT service management. Example objectives could be: find

two potential efficiencies in how we handle incidents (or some other process); provide a proposal relating to how automation can be used to handle password resets; investigate run book automation opportunities; increase the understanding of the customer-facing IT services concepts and present this information to the team.

- Host a vision and strategy session with a subset of both senior management and staff. Identify the desired result for the ITIL initiative and talk about how the organization can transition from the current state to the end result. Ask frontline employees in attendance to share the results of the session with their teams.
- Temporarily assign staff new roles and responsibilities that are associated with the project. Change their reporting structure, so they are a direct report of the project manager or project sponsor.
- Schedule a brainstorming session to focus on identifying pain points associated with existing operations and gathering ideas that can be used when determining ITIL-related improvements.

Stage two of Lewin's model is the **Change** phase. This stage is the most difficult. It is where the details of the changes are defined and implemented. The organization is moving toward a new way of doing business.

In this stage, people are directly impacted by the changes that occur. Significant engagement, coaching, training, and communication needs to take place. The desired end state is known, as it was needed for the initial analysis that occurred in the unfreeze stage. The change stage involves building the path from the current state to the desired end state.

Project plans, organizational change plans, and communication plans will all be developed and implemented during the change stage. Throughout this book, substantial guidance has been provided on engaging staff in determining the changes necessary for success. Engaging senior leaders, managers, and staff in the changes and reinforcing the required changes through using metrics and performance goals, is highly recommended.

Examples of techniques associated with the change phase include:

- Provide a safe environment for questions and making mistakes. The reaction of leadership when staff inquire about why a change is occurring, or how it should occur, will play a role in how comfortable staff members are with the change. In addition, mistakes will be made as the changes occur. Provided the mistake was made in good faith, it is important to learn from the mistakes and, if possible, use them as an example of learning.

- Engage the staff in determining how the ITIL processes, services, and systems should work. While the overall strategy may have been decided at a higher level, the organization has staff that are doing the work every day. Provide them with an objective to design the process that achieves the defined end result.

- Design a development plan for each staff member to ensure that each has the skills necessary to perform their new responsibilities. Include assignments where they are required to use the training as part of their development.

- Create temporary assignments and/or restructure as necessary to accommodate the defined end result.

- Publicly display and report on service management metrics clearly showing the initial performance of the

3: Organizational Change Models

organization, as well as incremental changes associated with the improvements. Celebrate incremental improvements and analyze challenging areas.

The final stage is the **Freezing** phase where the changes that were implemented become normal and the environment becomes stable once again. In the world of IT, it is often short-lived as change is always taking place. Still, the new changes need to be solidly rooted in the organization.

With an ITIL initiative, this stage would involve maintaining the stability of metrics and ongoing accountability for meeting the metrics and objectives. Usually the project is over, but operations which include ITIL processes are taking place every day as a normal course of business. Perhaps performance objectives are routinely reviewed with staff; service level compliance is reviewed with the customer; change management effectiveness is reviewed by leadership; or the cost of services is reviewed during the budget cycle. Whatever the metric, it occurs as part of normal operations.

In addition to metrics, corporate policies, values, and practices should be updated to reflect the changes, including performance and reward systems and job descriptions. Finally, take time to celebrate the end result, so the team feels that their hard work is appreciated.

McKinsey 7S model®

The McKinsey 7S model was introduced by Tom Peters and Robert Waterman (1984) who were consultants associated with the firm of McKinsey and Company. (For further information also see: *www.mindtools.com* and Pascale, 1991). The goal is to assess the current state of an organization; compare the current state to the desired state to identify gaps; and then create a plan to address the gaps. A core concept of the model is that for a change to be successful, the seven areas addressed by the model need to be properly aligned which results in each element reinforcing the other six.

ITIL provides specific guidance regarding understanding the desired state prior to the current state. The material in this book is not meant to reflect the guidance provided within the ITIL materials. It merely reflects another approach to completing this analysis.

The 7S model is often used at a strategic level for planning an ITIL initiative. When combined with other more employee-focused change methodologies, it becomes easier to address both strategy and execution, ensuring a comprehensive view of the changes required.

When using McKinsey 7S for planning an organizational change associated with an ITIL initiative, identify the existing and desired states in the seven areas addressed by the McKinsey model. The elements of the model are dependent upon each other to fully address achieving the desired state, so it is important that all areas are evaluated and addressed. The seven elements of the McKinsey model are noted below.

Strategy

The plan required to achieve an organization's vision and meet the required overall objectives is the strategy. When considering strategy, it is important to look at the current state; the changing market or environment; where the organization needs to evolve in order to remain relevant or obtain a competitive advantage; and the timing required for the changes to occur.

Most likely, strategy discussions resulted in the ITIL initiative. As the ITIL project commences, additional in-depth strategy visioning sessions, to identify the desired end state as well as the journey to success, are often conducted as they identify success, potential obstacles, guiding principles, key stakeholders, and, usually, project participants. These sessions are also a key element associated with obtaining executive buy-in.

Structure

Every organization has an organizational structure. In the McKinsey model, the organizational chart and leadership structure is evaluated to determine if the existing structure will meet the needs of the business once the required changes are implemented.

For large-scale ITIL projects, it is common to see the structure of an organization change due to the implementation of formal processes. For example, new departments may be created when true problem management is adopted. Permanent governance structures may be established to ensure funds are allocated to developing or creating services that provide the highest value to the business.

Systems

Think of systems as the policies, processes, and procedures used by an organization to complete their day-to-day activities. Evaluating the existing state for how work is completed will most likely lead to questions about why specific tasks or processes are in place. It is common to implement processes and continue to tweak them, but, unless there is a specific initiative, companies rarely reevaluate a process from end to end. Evaluating the systems may lead to some additional ideas relating to process improvement.

With an ITIL-related initiative, a fair amount of time should be spent evaluating the existing state, outlining the desired state, and identifying how to address the gap. What is the outcome desired from the initiative? Consider the organizational change aspects. For example, if the desired outcome includes building a culture that values continual improvement, what steps could be taken to move from the current state to the future desired state? Numerous possibilities exist, such as publicizing metrics, incentivizing process improvement suggestions and outcomes, creating new objectives for performance appraisals, routine focused improvement initiatives, or discussion groups.

When evaluating systems, consideration should be given to the organizational change required to be successful with the new or changed processes that are being implemented.

Shared values

Many organizations define core values for the company. If the core values are not defined, they are usually fairly evident in the culture and work ethic.

With the McKinsey 7S model, the shared values are reevaluated due to the IT service management initiative. Should the values change? If the values are not documented, do they need to be documented for the IT division, or the company? Documenting and publicizing the core values helps to build the foundation for a cohesive team that understands the guiding principles of the company. Understanding the values further assists employees in decision making and reduces some of the personal agendas that may exist.

Do the shared values change as a result of the ITIL initiative? If so, how do they change? It may be difficult to define in some organizations. If the organization is now focused on meeting service levels, a value may exist regarding providing timely, consistent customer service to support the business need. The IT investment strategy may be changing, so perhaps a new IT core value is created around investing in the right technology and resources to support business outcomes.

In some companies, documenting or changing the core values may be too political and, therefore, it may be out of scope for the project. Even if the formal work does not take place to make these changes, the necessary outcomes should still be considered in the communication plans and project tasks. Communication with staff members that certain behaviors are valued by the project and, subsequently, the IT organization can still influence the shared values of the organization.

Skills

When considering the organizational change requirements for the ITIL initiative, create a three-step model which includes skills that exist today, skills that are important during the journey, and skills required in the desired state.

Rather than starting with the existing state, consider the desired state first.

Start with the **desired state**. What skills are required to maintain and continuously improve the end result? Examples of desired skills may include: ITIL specific knowledge, such as a general understanding of IT service management, vocabulary, processes, or certification; analytical skills; communication skills; application-related knowledge; process mapping; analytics; specific technical skills; conflict resolution; continual improvement; auditing and/or auditing certification; and presentation skills.

Consider the **journey** to the desired state. What skills are required during the journey? The journey may require skills that are strong in a specific area, such as negotiation. Once the implementation and stabilization period is complete, the skill sets required during the journey are most likely still necessary, only the depth and breadth of skill in a specific area may be lessened. Examples of skills required during the journey include: strong negotiation; organizational change; active listening; communication skills including the ability to convey complex information in a manner that is easy to understand; a structured approach to decision making; and tenacity.

Finally, what skills **exist** in the organization today? In the organization today, every individual has a skill set. It may or may not require development for the journey and to effectively sustain and improve the end result. Define the existing skill sets and identify the gaps that need to be filled for both the journey and the desired state. Evaluate who will fill the various roles identified and determine where gaps exist during the journey and in the desired state. Consider how those gaps should be filled. If possible, develop objectives for each individual to develop in the required area, including training- and work-related tasks to develop their skills.

The eventual skills required in the **desired state** may not be as important during the **journey** and vice versa. Temporary responsibilities may be identified during the journey, as individuals within the company may have key skills to success in this area. It is quite common to temporarily assign the role of change evangelist, sponsor, change agent, and even process ownership during an ITIL process implementation.

Style

Consider the effectiveness of leadership within the organization. What behaviors do they exhibit? Overall, are leaders successful? Is there a sense of teamwork in the IT organization, or merely silos that function together?

When evaluating style, consideration should be given to how the project can leverage the existing style to its benefit and what changes are needed. If the organization and leadership has a collaborative style, conducting focus groups, or gathering feedback through surveys, may be an easy task. Engagement of individuals in the project may merely be an exercise in understanding their workload and determining how to integrate the project, and end result, into their existing responsibilities.

It becomes more difficult if the leadership has a contentious style, or if there is a lack of communication amongst the leadership team. The leadership in each organization is unique and, therefore, the methods employed relating to style will vary. In an organization where leadership has its challenges, the efforts to effectively leverage the positive aspects of style will require considerably more resources. There will be a substantial number of individual conversations to gain the trust and support of the project and some of the group meetings may take additional time as significant debate may occur. The individual meetings will be crucial to success and these meetings should occur prior to group discussions. It is also important to share only the level of information that is necessary for the audience, as leadership with a contentious style often will become mired in the details.

The style of leadership is difficult to change unless there is authority to do so through the use of performance objectives and other HR means. In this area, it is recommended that the style of key individuals be defined and strategies for ensuring trust, adoption, and support be defined with tactics, and tasks for leveraging and managing individuals built into the project plan.

Staff

The staff element of the McKinsey 7S model relates to understanding what is required for the staff to be successful. This element includes ensuring the right competencies exist, the organizational structure is appropriate, and that staff are prepared to take on their new responsibilities.

In reviewing the organization, what characteristics are present in the existing staff? Are there distinctive qualities about the team? It is important to consider any staff or roles, or even departments that are pertinent to the project. For example, if one of the affected teams is outsourced, this is a relevant detail that must be considered during the project, as there may be contractual issues to consider.

Consideration should also be given to the organizational structure and whether changes are necessary. Is a new department or team required? How will it be formed? Does the organization support matrix management, or should process-related roles be consolidated under one leader?

During the analysis of skills, what gaps were identified and how are those gaps going to be filled? What roles are needed now that the ITIL processes are being implemented or changing? Are additional personnel needed?

Evaluate the staff aspects of the initiative and plan for organizational- and staff-related tasks in the ITIL project plan and assign accountability for each of the tasks.

When using the McKinsey 7S organizational change model, it is important to note that this is an iterative process. Throughout the lifecycle of the project, each element should be periodically evaluated. Shared values are central to all of the other elements of the model. If shared values change, there is a ripple effect experienced in all other areas, with each element requiring evaluation once again.

After identifying the existing and desired states in all seven areas, conduct a gap analysis to determine what areas need to be addressed. Once the gaps are identified, planning can take place regarding how to address the gaps noted in each of the seven areas. A project plan, including organizational change activities and a communication plan, can be developed. To ensure an effective ITIL process and a smoother change initiative, frontline staff and leadership engagement in the McKinsey 7S activities is critical. At a minimum, gap analysis results should be shared and updated with feedback, however, the process and effectiveness of the organizational change initiative will be considerably enhanced by the participation of staff and leadership.

A recurring theme throughout this book is the importance of metrics. With every change model, baseline metrics should be understood. Routine reporting and monitoring of metrics should occur to ensure the changes required are on track. Without metrics, it is difficult to know if the changes are having the desired effect.

To ensure all seven areas remain aligned, it is recommended that additional reviews of all seven areas occur at key points throughout the project. As noted earlier, when using the 7S model, it is crucial that all elements are aligned to recognize the full benefit of the changes. Conducting periodic reviews of all seven elements, and adjusting as necessary, will minimize the risk associated with changes in one area. In addition, changes to the shared values element may result in a substantial change in the other areas, so significant monitoring should occur in this area.

Kotter's eight-step model for change

The eight-step model for change was created by John Kotter (1996). It focuses on building employee support and understanding along with strengthening change and accountability. Use of the model begins early in an ITIL project, usually in the initiation stage, by creating a sense of urgency and understanding with employees which occurs either in tandem, or shortly before, assembling a project team. As noted by the name, the model has eight key elements.

1. Establish a sense of urgency

When using the Kotter model, the first step is to establish a sense of urgency about the changes. This element of the model is foundational as the purpose of the project is communicated. Communication includes why the project needs to occur and sells the benefits to employees. The purpose of the communication is to convince the employees that it is in the best interest of the company and the employee to make this change. As noted in *Chapter 1*, the value proposition can be used to create this communication.

The Kotter model includes a strong focus on accountability and the groundwork is often laid within the very early stages. It includes not only selling the changes, but also identifying consequences of not changing, both in the short and long term. What is the impact to the company, division, department, and employee if the changes do not occur?

Examples of potential items to include in the communication include: how IT supports the business today and why the ITIL project is required to effectively support it tomorrow; IT budget impacts linked to necessary outcomes from the project; technology-related challenges with language regarding how ITIL can help to decrease the impact; and the benefits of the ITIL model on IT service, along with an explanation of why the change is necessary.

2. Create a guiding coalition

The second phase of the model includes formation of a team to execute the change. Often referred to as a **coalition for change**, this step includes forming the project team and identifying key change-related roles within the company. In _Chapter 7_, we'll discuss key roles, such as the change evangelist, change agent, and sponsor. Some critical skills for change-related roles are also identified.

Clear accountability for the overall change, as well as smaller change-related tasks are also defined and communicated. Lines of authority and boundaries are established. For example, if changes are occurring to operating level agreements, but the responsible teams are not responding appropriately, who owns the issue – the Service Level Manager or Line Management? Who is accountable for employees changing their behavior?

When determining lines of authority and boundaries, it is important to consider who owns the success of a particular aspect of the project, as well as who is responsible for providing employees with the tools and knowledge they need to be successful. Defining both roles will assist in determining both authority and boundaries.

3. Develop a vision and strategy

As with any change, a vision should be created. The Kotter model includes a specific step to define the desired end result, thereby allowing employees to understand what the changes should accomplish. It provides grounding for the team when making decisions about the changes necessary.

When creating a vision, attention should be paid to how the vision links to the overall health of the company, division, department, and employee. Once the end state is defined, the project team, in partnership with leadership, will determine the steps necessary to achieve the end state vision. There are two potential paths to take in this regard. The first path involves taking the end state vision for the overall ITIL initiative and defining the organizational change required to achieve the end state and, further, identifying organizational change-related tasks to progress to the end state.

The second path is to identify an end state vision for organizational change. For example, the desired end state may be to have an organization that embraces process and continual improvement. Once the end state vision is determined, the behavior changes necessary to support achieving the end state should be identified, further drilling down to determine the tasks necessary to change the behavior.

Both the first and second path can effectively achieve the desired outcome. The options are noted in this section as those planning for the changes may become confused regarding organizational change models versus general project planning. It is common to use the project's desired end state, or the first path noted above, however, if large-scale organizational change is necessary, defining the end state vision for organizational change may be a more prudent path, due to the depth and breadth of change required.

4. Communicate the change vision

Another foundational element of the model is to ground the vision and changes with leadership first, ensuring

3: Organizational Change Models

leadership support, understanding, and responsibility for the vision. Depending on the size of the company, some of the leaders may have been engaged in defining the vision. Communication to leadership should start at the highest level; however, others who were engaged may conduct smaller more focused sessions with departments, or one-to-one sessions with key leaders. The goal of the leadership conversations is to ensure understanding, allowing the leaders to effectively support and manage conversations when employees have questions.

After establishing support with leadership, broader communication should occur in the company, as well as with those affected, again focusing on the value proposition of the vision for the company, division, department, and employee. Included in the communication should be the reasoning behind the change, as well as the potential detrimental effects on the overall business, if the change doesn't occur.

All of the communication elements of Kotter's model should be planned for using a communication plan which links to the organizational change and project plans. Additional guidance regarding the use of communication plans and organizational change plans is provided in *Chapter 6*.

5. Empower broad-based action

Determine what changes need to occur to ensure individuals are empowered. Quickly address issues which prevent progress. Create a safe environment to discuss failures, or aspects of the changes that did not go as planned. Celebrate the discussions regarding challenges by publicizing initial setbacks and plans to continue forward momentum.

Identify those who are resistant to change and determine a course of action which minimizes their impact on the team and the project. Publicly and privately reward those who embrace the change, remembering that recognition can occur in many forms and it does not always involve giving monetary compensation.

Hold people accountable not only for accomplishing their tasks, but also for providing support to the project. Accountability for the change is vital within the Kotter model. Celebrate a spirit of learning and progress, but also quickly act when finger pointing or blaming occurs, as it is rarely productive. In *Chapter 5*, additional guidance is provided regarding holding people accountable.

6. Create short-term wins

Establish short- and long-term goals for the ITIL initiative. Every project has short-term wins. Within an ITIL initiative, short-term wins can usually be found within incident management, request fulfillment, and problem management, although short-term wins will exist in almost every lifecycle and capability area.

Create baseline metrics for all of the goals identified. To create excitement regarding the changes, focus on the short-term wins and successes. Market the success to the entire organization by publicizing both the tangible metric-based progress and intangible progress. Publicly reward those making significant contributions toward the change.

Long-term goals are often significant milestones in the journey to improvement. Promotional activities and celebrations should be planned to recognize the achievement of milestones. Publicly displayed metrics along with communication regarding the project and the outcomes will often create the necessary behavior changes to support the project.

7. *Consolidate gains and produce more change*

Within this phase, the focus is on improving the short-term wins. Identify employees making substantial contributions toward change, to determine how to leverage their influence and ideas to continue improving upon existing changes. Reward persistence, tenacity, and out-of-the-box thinking using both corporate reward systems and unique project-related reward opportunities.

Complete lessons learned for difficult aspects of the change and modify the course of action for future changes. Add new people to the core team, to bring in a new perspective and to further engage employees in the changes taking place. Focus on continual service improvement within the project and begin to operationalize the concept of continual improvement within the organization.

When evaluating employee contributions to the changes, some staff members are often identified as making substantial contributions. It is common for leaders to want to use the energy and brainpower of star performers by providing them with additional opportunities. While these opportunities can be quite beneficial for both the company and the employee, be careful not to overload the star performer with too many tasks, projects, and meetings. Balance leveraging their ideas and ability to influence others with their workload.

See *True stories from the frontline* at the end of this chapter for a related story about an overloaded employee.

8. Anchor new approaches in the culture

The Kotter model includes a final step relating to anchoring the change within the company culture. Within this step, the change outcomes are embedded. This is accomplished by updating company values, practices, and policies. Corporate metrics should also be updated to reflect any new metrics available as a result of the change.

Within this phase of the model, service level targets, agreements, underpinning contracts, service costs, the service catalog, as well as IT-specific policies and objectives are formally updated, signed off, and published.

Anchoring the change includes additional steps to reinforce accountability for the change and continual improvement. While change-related objectives may have been included in the employee performance appraisal, metrics for ongoing operations and process performance improvements associated with the recent changes should now be added.

How can an organizational change model help?

As noted at the beginning of this chapter, there are numerous organizational change models. Significant research has been conducted to determine how to manage organizational change and the impact that people can have on the success of a change. The models noted in this publication can be used individually, or combined, to effectively address the organizational change needs of any ITIL initiative.

Even the best project manager or leader can end up in a situation where their initiative fails, or doesn't achieve the desired end result. Perhaps planning occurred and the technical- and process-related changes occurred on time and within budget, yet the organization didn't respond as expected, or the results that were anticipated weren't realized. Understanding that organizational change can impact success and, further, taking the time to consider and plan for the behavior changes necessary by the employee, is an important step toward maximizing the opportunity for success.

Selecting an organizational change model and incorporating the core concepts into tasks for an organizational change and communication plan, will reduce potential challenges faced by the project in meeting the success criteria identified. Planning, key roles and aspects of change, and core skills are important components of successful change; these are covered in future chapters of this book.

True stories from the frontline: an overloaded employee

I was working with a company that was undergoing massive change. The marketplace was shifting and the company needed to make substantial changes to accommodate the marketplace, reduce cost, comply with new regulations, and maintain their competitive advantage. This was the state of the health insurance market during healthcare reform.

Within the company, everything was changing. New products were being introduced. Projects were underway to address new regulations. Process efficiency initiatives were underway and automation was pursued. Restructuring was occurring at the highest level and cascading changes emerged as a result.

The company had some employees with significant tenure. Tenured employees were used to accommodating changes in various departments, often employing manual methods to handle exceptions that an improvement in another area created for them. The changes occurring required new ways of thinking and a firm stance on employing automation without numerous exceptions. It was going to take a while for the tenured employees to adjust to the new way of working.

While I was responsible for initiating a fair number of the process and automation projects, I was often allocated to other projects, or required to engage in other initiatives to ensure that efficiency gains previously recognized were maintained or improved upon.

My standard workweek was somewhere between fifty and sixty hours. When I planned a vacation, I would often work weekends for several months leading up to my time off in order to ensure everything was in place, so I could relax. When I returned it would take about a month for my schedule and workload to return to a barely manageable level.

I was in a multi-day planning meeting when I saw the tsunami coming. With new projects, speed to market being reduced for new products, and schedules and timelines for existing initiatives being fast tracked, a huge wave of work was heading my way. As the work that my team was doing on process improvement and automation touched almost every system and team in the company, we were going to be in the middle of everything. If the company wanted the work to be successful, a new product or product change couldn't go to market without our involvement. Every system change in every department would also require our engagement.

I created plans to address the workload that was clearly on the horizon. New job descriptions and organizational charts were created. During this planning, I attempted to address my workload, as well as the workload of my team. When I addressed the issue with my boss and presented the plans, I was asked to hold off on moving forward until a leadership offsite meeting. Major restructuring was expected and resources may be available as a result. I expressed reluctance in waiting; I was concerned about the impending storm of work.

The leadership offsite meeting was two full days in another city. By the time the offsite meeting occurred, I was already so busy that I could only fly in for about four hours of the meeting. During the meeting, additional new projects were discussed. I repeatedly expressed concerns about the amount of change already taking place and I managed to convince the leadership team to minimize the number of new projects. The meeting yielded nothing in terms of additional resources for my team.

When I returned to the office the next day, I worked with HR to post the job descriptions and implement the changes I had identified six weeks prior. Hiring resources and restructuring takes time and every day my schedule and workload became worse. It took about four months to find the resources I needed and they still had to come up to speed and understand the complexity of the environment and existing projects.

By the time I hired some of the key resources necessary, I was already in a situation that was untenable. I worked well over sixty hours per week. I stopped tracking my hours, but I can tell you that I worked nights and weekends often coming into the office at five am. Most people are unable to truly comprehend just how bad my workload was even when I describe it. I was in 20 to 30 meetings in an eight- to ten-hour day. I was booked six weeks in advance. Emergencies, or a crisis of any kind, caused incredible havoc with the schedule. The meetings already on the books were not superfluous. They were all necessary. My administrator spent the majority of her time scheduling and rescheduling meetings, seeking assistance from other resources to help with her own workload. Lunch was delivered to me in meetings. Slides and projectors were setup prior to the start of meetings, so I could literally walk in the door and start a presentation. When I went to the restroom, people walked with me as they needed input and it was a rare opportunity to have my undivided attention. Of course, going to the restroom meant I was late for my next meeting.

I received 400+ e-mails per day. My administrator would review them and provide me with a one-page summary at the end of every day. She would note the e-mails requiring an answer, as well as those with associated deadlines. Anything not on that list would have to wait about a month for a response. She would also give me my schedule for the next day and any documents associated with travel. I answered e-mails and did actual work in the evenings and on weekends. If I needed to travel for work, I traveled in the evenings and on weekends.

I tried to meet with my direct reports every one to two weeks. Their meetings would be rescheduled numerous times. I made sure they had what they needed, as I instant messaged them while in other meetings. If I signed out of instant messaging, or if I didn't answer, the text messaging would start.

Prior to the tsunami of work, I often communicated with my boss that I thought we should look at ways to manage my workload. When all of the new initiatives affected my workload, my boss often commented that my role and responsibilities were absolutely out of control, yet necessary to ensure success. During these conversations, I would reiterate that something needed to change.

After about a year of this crazy schedule and workload, I realized that I was done. I'd had enough. It happened one evening when my boss stopped by my office. She complained about being at the office so late. She proceeded to tell me that she had just volunteered to create a plan for a current crisis and develop a long-range strategic plan associated with managing a specific type of work. As she was talking, I realized that while she wasn't openly saying it, she had just volunteered me to take on additional work. She didn't understand the processes and technology enough to do the task. She was expecting me to handle it.

I told her that she was well aware of my workload and that I hoped she wasn't expecting me to handle it, as I couldn't take on another project. She looked at me as though I had two heads and promptly asked me to create a plan for how the company could handle it if I could not take on the project.

I knew she respected me and she knew the job would get done, but in her world, my workload was never going to be a consideration. While she wanted me to complete both the crisis and strategic plan, I had other corporate initiatives requiring my attention. In that moment, I made a decision that it was time to find another job. I drew out a plan on the whiteboard for managing both the crisis and strategic plan. She suggested another leader in her organization handle it, but asked me to serve as a mentor. I agreed, but knew that I would be required to step in if the project was going to be successful.

While I started looking for a job, I attended another leadership retreat. During this session, I ended up owning a restructuring of compensation and bonus plans. I had nothing to do with HR, but this was assigned by the senior executive team. An HR person was sitting at the same table with me. It was yet another task on an already overloaded "to do" list.

I was well known for driving change in the organization. My opinion was respected and valued, which is why I frequently was assigned projects outside of my realm. I was creative with funding and I drove some changes that saved the company millions of dollars with only minimal investment. My sphere of influence was significant. People often chose to wait two months to get on my calendar, rather than work with my boss or others. The leaders in the company recognized my accomplishments and they wanted to leverage my skills and abilities in a number of areas. What they failed to recognize, or chose to ignore, was my workload.

It is great to have talented people on the team. In order to keep them, attention must be paid to their work/life balance. Every leadership job requires that schedules and workloads flex to meet demand. Effective leadership ensures that employee skills, talents, and abilities are maximized, while not taking advantage, or overloading them to the point where their personal life is non-existent.

I left this company approximately ninety days after I decided it was time to go. I never finished the compensation project that was assigned to me by the senior executives. By the time the project was assigned, I was in the final interviewing stages with two other companies. I was offered both opportunities and chose the one that was right for me at the time.

I learned a lot during my time with this employer. While I was always cognizant of my employees' work/life balance, I take extra steps to monitor it now. I expect them to work as necessary to get the job done and it often requires well over forty hours, but the schedule flexes. I develop and engage different employees in different initiatives. I attempt to balance the work across the team. Some employees are higher performing than others, but I still manage to leverage their talents while not overwhelming them.

To keep good employees, we must provide them with challenges, recognize their accomplishments, and utilize them in a manner that benefits the company. We also have to ensure they are happy and address their concerns, even if it means they cannot participate in every project.

CHAPTER 4: SELECTING A CHANGE MODEL

There are many change models. Some are more complex than others. In this book, we've reviewed five different models each focusing on organizational change, yet in some cases, they take a very different approach. Which change model is right for the ITIL initiative?

- ADKAR which addressed:
  - o awareness
  - o desire
  - o knowledge
  - o ability
  - o reinforcement.

- Six Change which spoke of:
  - o education and communication
  - o participation and involvement
  - o facilitation and support
  - o negotiation and agreement
  - o manipulation and co-option
  - o explicit and implicit coercion.

- Freeze Change which included:
  - o preparing the organization for change
  - o the actual change
  - o freezing the changes.

- McKinsey 7S which involved addressing:
  - o strategy
  - o structure
  - o systems
  - o shared values
  - o skills

o style
o staff.

- Kotter's eight-step model focusing on:
  o establishing a sense of urgency
  o creating a guiding coalition
  o developing a vision and strategy
  o communicating the change vision
  o empowering broad-based action
  o creating short-term wins
  o consolidating gains and producing more change
  o anchoring new approaches in the culture.

Which model is right for the organization and/or project?

To determine the right change model for the project, evaluate the benefits and disadvantages of each model while considering the organization. Each model has its strengths and weaknesses and, therefore, the models should be evaluated based on what is needed in the organization. The strengths and weaknesses noted are based on the author's opinion, having used the models in various organizational change-related scenarios.

When considering which method is right for the organization, it is important to evaluate the project itself, as well as the extent of the changes relating to people, processes, and technology in the existing organization. In addition, consideration should be given to the leadership philosophies and strengths, as well as taking a realistic view of the time and resources available to address organizational change. Often, it is beneficial to use a hybrid model to effectively address change in the organization, as one model does not sufficiently manage all aspects of the change.

ADKAR

The ADKAR model is relatively easy to use, yet comprehensive in helping to prepare for the ITIL process changes that are taking place. The model addresses strong communication from project inception through implementation, to ensure that staff are aware of the changes and how the changes impact the organization, as well as the individual staff member. Use of the ADKAR model requires a focus on ensuring employees are successful in their role, as it requires planning for both the knowledge and ability of the staff members. Reinforcement activities are also addressed to embed the changes during the project implementation.

When substantial change is occurring, leadership should engage in the awareness, desire, and reinforcement components of the model when planning tasks necessary to address these aspects of organizational change. In addition, leadership engagement is required during the actual execution of tasks associated with these areas. Employees often look to leadership for guidance and support during times of substantial change and, therefore, patient, understanding leadership is required to effectively address these areas during execution of the associated tasks.

The ADKAR model is easily applied to any size of change; however, it strongly focuses on identifying the tasks necessary to support the employee through the changes. It does not effectively address strategy for achieving the desired outcome. Often the strategy for IT service management is defined through other mechanisms in the organization, so this may not be an issue. In *Chapter 1*, additional guidance was provided on defining the value proposition for the initiative. The outcome of the discussions around value proposition may also suffice depending on the organization, as well as the size and complexity of the changes taking place.

Six Change

The Six Change model includes some planning components, as well as techniques, for managing resistance to change. While education, communication, participation, and involvement are addressed, techniques such as negotiation, co-option, and coercion are included as well. Techniques for managing resistance are not a substantial component of any of the other models noted and, therefore, even if the model is not used in its entirety, the techniques should be considered for use with other organizational change models.

If the changes occurring within the organization are fairly contained and/or the individuals impacted are known to resist change, the Six Change model is usually a good fit. Leaders within the organization can easily understand and apply the techniques noted to manage resistance, provided they are not conflict avoidant. The explicit and implicit coercion technique is key to minimizing resistance to change when team members have strong personalities and are known to resist change. This technique requires leaders to engage in difficult conversations and to hold each team member accountable for their actions, as well as attitudes.

Strategy associated with the ITIL initiative and organizational change is not a component of this model, however, as noted within the ADKAR section, the strategy may already be defined, or use of the guidance provided in *Chapter 1* relating to the definition of the value proposition may provide enough information, so this is not an issue.

As the Six Change model splits the focus areas to address both planning and techniques, care should be taken to ensure that there is a healthy focus on determining the tactics necessary to achieve the desired outcome. As the model includes three planning-related focus areas, application of the model sometimes requires a conscious effort to place the right amount of emphasis in this area.

Freeze Change

The Freeze Change model is a simplistic model which focuses on taking employees out of their comfort zone in order to facilitate change. The three core aspects of this model rely heavily on leadership, as taking people out of their comfort zone can often cause significant churn in the organization. Strong, trusted leaders are required to provide guidance and support to ensure the existing work occurs without issue and employees are encouraged to provide ideas and thoughts on how to improve existing processes.

This model is often best utilized in small to mid-sized organizations, as managing the upheaval that potentially occurs within the organization may become unwieldy in larger IT divisions.

One of the key benefits of this model is the out-of-the-box thinking that can occur when staff are out of their comfort zone. If the IT organization is facing complex challenges and is open to potential creative solutions from those actually completing the work, this model may be a good fit.

While the model is simple, IT organizations have some very intelligent and innovative individuals on the team. Once there is an understanding of the business challenge, ingenious solutions are often identified by IT staff. If these ideas are then implemented as part of the ITIL initiative, support from the team becomes easier, as they were engaged in determining a solution.

While the Freeze Change concept is simple, it can be difficult to use for in-depth planning. Consideration may be given to using this model to spark innovation, while using another model to plan for execution.

McKinsey 7S

The McKinsey 7S model is an exhaustive model that includes understanding not only strategy, but the strengths and weaknesses of the team, as well as the shared values of the organization. Each component of the model builds on the next allowing for comprehensive planning.

This model can be used regardless of the size of the organization, however, it is comprehensive, and, often, a change in one area of the model requires that all steps be reevaluated, as every area is interconnected. Therefore, consideration should be given to the size and complexity of the changes when using this model. If the IT service management initiative is a comprehensive rollout of ITIL processes within a large organization, and there is recognition that resources are needed to address organizational change, this model may be a good fit.

Corporate shared values are at the center of the model. All of the other aspects may affect the values and, therefore, tactics need to be considered for influencing both the emotional and rational aspects of change.

In larger organizations, consideration of this model may also occur due to the name recognition associated with McKinsey. Politics can affect the success of change initiatives. While other change models may not be well known, the McKinsey name, at times, will carry some level of credibility and, therefore, it may be easier to sell this model in larger organizations.

Kotter's eight-step model for change

The Kotter model focuses on acceptance, preparation for change, and continual improvement. It is an easy to understand model which addresses early awareness and urgency, as well as planning, accountability, vision, and employee empowerment.

The model can be used for any size initiative and it works well in any size organization. Significant emphasis is placed on the planning aspects of change. To ensure effectiveness, the eight steps included in the model should be followed in order.

Accountability is core to success when executing this model. It is a strong focus in the early steps and, therefore, consideration should be given to the culture of the existing organization. Kotter's model requires a strong, cohesive management team to effectively achieve the desired end result. Is there a focus on accountability in day-to-day operations? Does the management team have a strong bond? If so, this model may be a good fit.

Also, when applying the model, tactics to influence attitudes and behaviors at the time of execution may become difficult to identify. If this occurs, consider using Kotter's model in tandem with ADKAR or Six Change, in order to recognize tasks which can influence adoption.

As noted at the beginning of this chapter, each organizational change model discussed has strengths and weaknesses. The organization, leadership, scope, and complexity should all be evaluated when choosing a model for use with an ITIL initiative. The author recommends using a hybrid approach, including aspects from various models to ensure comprehensive planning and execution is addressed based on the needs of the project.

True stories from the frontline: success was planned

If you think about a corporate merger involving four separate companies operating in four different states in a heavily regulated industry, you can imagine that potentially, massive change is going to take place. Now, imagine these companies will continue to operate as separate entities, only they will merge to one set of systems and create one, single set of processes for daily operations. During my career, I worked in this situation. I was accountable for operational processes and the systems required to support four separate companies.

The project spanned multiple years, however, the timeline was accelerated rather suddenly by eighteen months in an effort to reduce the cost and, quite frankly, so the company could move on. The project was so large it had been a corporate focus for far too long, often diverting attention from other relevant, business activities.

Everyone in this mid-sized organization was impacted by the changes occurring. We were moving to one common set of systems and processes, so nobody was immune to the changes that were taking place.

With the accelerated schedule, some amount of chaos was bound to occur, regardless of how much planning took place. Key stakeholders and sponsors of the project were valiant in their attempts to prepare and manage organizational change. I was accountable for ensuring that thousands of employees could effectively do their jobs with every phased implementation associated with this project. In tandem, the company was releasing new products and existing customers needed to continue receiving high-quality service.

We employed the ADKAR model to plan for the necessary changes. For each phase of the project, we planned communications, training, activities, knowledge, and reinforcement activities to address all five aspects of the ADKAR model. We executed based on our project plans.

When senior leaders traveled to various locations, we met with teams and talked about the changes. Roadshows were undertaken to demonstrate new system functionality. Managers were given talking points for their various meetings. Newsletters were sent weekly to update everyone about recent occurrences, challenge areas, and next steps.

As mentioned earlier, there were times when chaos was bound to occur. One department apparently did not remember their agreement to handle some regulatory changes a specific way. They continued with their existing processes when the changes occurred, rather than making the changes required so the 1,000+ call center agents could effectively communicate about the changes.

When this problem occurred, it could have created widespread issues. While there were some challenges, overall the employees managed them well. They were informed about the changes. They went to their managers to talk through the problems; these managers knew who to turn to about any issues. Communication about problems occurred quickly and workarounds were put in place for the call center. A detailed explanation of the issue was provided to those directly involved in the project, as well as the entire leadership team. A team was formed to fix the existing problems and the process issue was corrected.

It was natural for people, myself included, to stop and grumble for a few minutes about the department that forgot to implement the changes required for regulatory issues. Additional time was required to fix the problem and it was time that we really didn't have to spend working on this issue. Nevertheless, we didn't focus on the negatives. The team came together to figure out how to fix the problem quickly. We communicated and made sure people had the ability to do their jobs both during the interim problem and, ultimately, long term.

The frontline teams who were affected didn't focus on the issue either. They recognized the problem and they moved on. They had confidence in the communication that would come about how to handle specific calls. They knew that we would handle the problem and provide them with workarounds as soon as we could.

The confidence from this team was a direct result of our planning for the organizational changes and the use of the ADKAR model. They knew what changes were occurring and when. They knew what resources were available to them. They wanted to be involved. They pulled as much information as we pushed to them about the project. The communication about the project was strong and the training and reinforcement activities were vast.

The use of an organizational change model for planning and, further, in execution, wasn't really an option when dealing with changes of this magnitude. It was a requirement and it proved invaluable to the overall success of the project.

CHAPTER 5: ACCOUNTABILITY

Regardless of which change method or model is used, it is easy to overlook a key aspect of organizational change that is critical to success. It is under-emphasized in the various change models and, in some cases, not addressed at all. It is accountability.

Without visible accountability, the changes being implemented will only partially be successful, if they are successful at all.

So, how does one define accountability? Take a few minutes now to really think about it. Are you holding people accountable? What does it mean to hold someone accountable? Are you an accountable person? When was the last time, when something didn't go right, that you said: "I should have done ..."; "it is my fault"?

Ultimately, the sponsor or project manager for the ITIL implementation is accountable for the end result. This does not mean that project participants are non-existent, or that they do not bear some responsibility. They may even be responsible for task completion or day-to-day operations, but, ultimately, who is accountable for the project?

Have you ever met someone who just seemed to blame everyone else when things went wrong? Nothing was ever their fault. They might have been a manager, or even a politician, but they were never responsible for a negative outcome. It was always someone on the team, or in the community. These individuals are great examples of individuals who are not accountable for their actions, or projects/initiatives that are being managed by them. We

5: Accountability

actually foster this behavior by allowing them to blame others when they are ultimately responsible. There may be examples of this behavior within the organization. Some organizations foster such behavior by allowing leaders to blame team members for various issues, while failing to recognize a pattern which may relate to a leadership issue.

Without accountability at the highest level of the change initiative, it will be difficult to truly realize the desired outcomes.

So, how do you foster accountability? It starts with you. Are you accountable? When was the last time something didn't go right? Did you blame others or take responsibility? What did you learn from the experience?

A critical piece of accountability is our learning for various experiences. When something doesn't go as planned, or the outcome isn't as expected, while it is okay to dissect the situation and determine where the difficulties occurred and who contributed to the issue, we shouldn't miss the most critical step. How did we contribute to the issue? Whether it was failing to recognize the problem; a lack of communication; or not realizing the politics associated with the project; there is always an opportunity for us to learn. By dissecting the problem and going one step further to ask how we contributed to the problem and then truly approaching this question with an emphasis on learning, rather than blaming ourselves, it is surprising how much insight we can gain and, going forward, we will be less likely to face similar challenges.

You've learned, but now you need to help others. How can you hold others accountable? We often have to manage upwards, sideways, and downwards.

5: Accountability

Sometimes, holding others accountable is as easy as changing the questions we ask. Instead of asking, "What went wrong?" you could ask, "What did you learn from this issue?" If someone begins blaming others for an issue, you could say, "I understand others contributed to the issue, but how could you have changed the outcome?" The trick is to stop the blaming and continuously focus on what can be learned.

Changing the conversation is just one step relating to accountability. We also need to take the time to understand what motivates people. It is easier said than done. Most people have good intentions, but their experiences and beliefs help shape their reactions. Ultimately, emotions relating to their experiences and beliefs drive their behavior. Emotions are complicated.

To understand what is driving behaviors, you can't accept the simple answer. Probing questions may be required. Asking a question that starts with "why" and then continuing to use "why" questions until you find the belief and understand the emotion, is one way to dig deeper in this area. If understanding emotions is of additional interest to you, there are many books on the topic of emotional intelligence which may be of assistance (for example, www.ihhp.com; Boyatzis, McKee and Goleman, 2004; Goleman, 2005).

Sometimes, after all of the learning and the probing, we just need to have a hard conversation about outcomes and/or behavior. To instill accountability, we really shouldn't shy away from these conversations. It is best to simply tackle them. We need to be accountable for having the conversation. It doesn't mean that we need to be confrontational. If you tend to avoid difficult conversations, it could be a contributor to some of the challenges you are facing with the ITIL implementation, or other projects.

As noted earlier in this chapter, we have to manage upwards, sideways, and downwards. Yes, that might mean a hard conversation with someone who has a higher rank than you in the organization, or maybe even a close peer. The following list provides some tips relating to conversations where you feel uncomfortable.

- Schedule the conversation. This may be the hardest part. By scheduling the conversation, you are making a commitment to have the conversation.
- Note the intended outcome. What do you want to happen as an outcome of the conversation? Is the conversation merely to tell someone how you feel? Do you want a change in behavior? Do you need some sort of activity completed by a certain date? It is critical to know going in what you want to happen as a result of the conversation.
- Outline the conversation, taking into consideration the intended outcome. What specifically do you want to talk about? Include examples.
- Determine your closing comments and reiterate expectations going forward. If you asked for a task to be completed, when should it be done? If you wanted a change in behavior, perhaps schedule a follow-up conversation to talk about progress. If it is appropriate, thank the person for taking the time to talk with you and for having what may have been an awkward discussion.

5: Accountability

True stories from the frontline: accountability

In the mid 1990s, I was accountable for service at an insurance company. The company had about 1,500 employees. In addition to insurance, they also sold software products. I was the face to the business and the executives when IT was having a bad day. If the company couldn't function due to significant degradation, or an outage, I was the one to explain it to the executive team and talk with the business areas. My team communicated with external customers. Since I was responsible for communications with the internal and external customers when things went wrong and my team felt the brunt of their unhappiness, I was also the final signoff for any changes to the production environment.

It was a very stressful job.

During my tenure with this employer, I encountered a director who seemed to fight me every step of the way. The company had many great leaders that I worked with every day, but one director and his team just kicked and screamed every time I asked about testing, back-out plans, scheduling, or any additional information about the change. When something went wrong though, they were the first team to call asking me to communicate with the customer about the issue, as they didn't want to be front and center. To be fair, they needed to be fixing the problem not communicating with the customer, but they also needed to work within the process and partner to ensure the change was implemented with minimal disruption.

The situation was very stressful. I sought assistance from my leadership with only minimal, short-lived success. My direct leadership just didn't want to take on the problem, yet praised me continuously for how I was handling it.

5: Accountability

The situation was making me miserable. This team was accountable for most of the changes in the environment. I was spending some portion of my time on a daily basis dealing with them.

I started interviewing with other companies. During one of those interviews, I observed a team that was high performing. When I asked what the key was to their success, their manager said they had a strong sense of accountability. When I talked to the team, they also referenced accountability. They said they spent time trying to learn from issues, rather than pointing a finger.

A light bulb went off for me and I spent some time considering my current situation. I started to consider how I could change the situation, rather than reacting to it and becoming stressed by every interaction with the team that was being so difficult. I asked myself what I could learn and how I could minimize the effect this team was having on me at work. If the company and leadership weren't going to change anything, one of two things would happen – either I could leave, or I could change how I reacted.

I began to analyze each interaction with the team. I realized that while I didn't have the authority to hold them accountable, I could create some reports to reflect all IT's success and challenges with change, problem, incident, and request management. The reports could further break down the statistics for each department, thereby shining a spotlight on issues. I routinely published these metrics for the executive team.

I also refrained from continuously discussing changes with the questionable team. I stated my position and refused signoff when appropriate. I let them know the steps they needed to take to obtain a signature. If they proceeded, I publicly asked the team for an analysis of what went wrong. I established a template for completing the analysis and I sent a summary to the CIO. All of the documents and conversations were completed without emotion. It was a job to protect the interests of the business and the customer, but it wasn't my life.

Over time, the public metrics and reporting on all of IT started to change the behavior of the problematic team. Once there was a spotlight on how changes were affecting production, even the executive team's behavior changed. The annual appraisal for the director in question now included objectives relating to managing incidents, problems, requests, and changes. His team also had some objectives relating to these processes, as well as attitude, and the overall impacts they had on the IT organization.

These changes did not occur overnight. It was several months before I really felt any relief, but my day did become less stressful. All of the changes resulted from my being accountable for changing a miserable situation. I couldn't change the situation, but I could change how I reacted to it and start thinking out of the box to find a solution.

I eventually did leave this company, but I've applied the lessons I learned relating to accountability everywhere I've worked since, and also in my personal life.

My experience with this employer taught me that I need to own every interaction. I need to learn what I can from every situation and apply what I learn to make things better. I need to be accountable. It really isn't that hard and it makes a tremendous difference.

CHAPTER 6: PLANNING

We've talked about organizational change, the value proposition, some change models, and the importance of accountability. How is all of this information brought together in a plan to address the organizational change required for an ITIL implementation?

In the course of this book, three plans have been mentioned. The project plan is meant to clarify, define, and track the course of the project. Project planning is a specialized area which is not covered in this book. It is assumed that a project plan is being used to manage the ITIL implementation. Project management is a best practice and is foundational to a successful large-scale implementation. While project plans add a lot of value, formal project plans are not always necessary, especially if the initiative is small. Regardless of the size of the project, organizational change should be considered and included as appropriate.

The organizational change plan is an input into the project plan, but it can stand on its own if a project plan is not being used. Similar to a project plan, the organizational change plan is a tool to help understand the steps necessary to achieve success and to track progress toward the end state.

Finally, the communication plan, in this instance, is an input into the organizational change plan and the project plan. As communication is vital to achieving success with organizational change, it requires some specific attention.

6: Planning

Organizational change plan

The organizational change plan is not complicated; however, it can take time to complete. The first step is to define what the desired state is in terms of what end result is required. A powerful tool which can help in this effort is gap analysis.

Gap analysis is a tool that when used appropriately, can assist with understanding how to move from the current to the desired state. It doesn't need to be complex. A simple five-column table will provide the structure necessary. The areas to explore in the table are as follows: the objective associated with the change, the desired state, the gaps between the current and desired states, the tasks necessary to move from the current state to the desired state, and finally, the success measures. When completing a gap analysis and determining the tasks to transition from the current to desired state, it is important to focus on the organizational change that needs to occur to be successful.

When creating an organizational change plan, the scope of the changes required needs definition. For each ITIL lifecycle stage, or for each of the ITIL processes, define the organizational change that is necessary for success. Use gap analysis to drill down to the lifecycle stages and conduct the same exercise for the processes that exist within the lifecycle. As noted, it can take time to complete a gap analysis. If merely one process is being completed, the task can be completed quickly. If a full ITIL implementation is within scope, gap analysis will need to be comprehensive, therefore, it will take significant time.

When completing the gap analysis, consider the level of change that is required to normal work activities, in order to move from the current state to the desired state.

6: Planning

Does a complete shift need to occur in the way business is conducted? What happens if the change is not realized? What is the risk? How fast does the organizational change need to occur? Are there incremental changes that can occur throughout the project?

The desired state is the outcome of the change. What behavior should be prevalent after the change has occurred? It is okay to have a long-term goal. Be sure that the tasks noted take steps to arrive at the end result. Several steps may be necessary, especially if a complete shift in behavior is desired. Large shifts, such as improving morale or forming partnerships between departments, may take some time and the planning associated with cultural-related shifts can be substantial.

Objective	Desired state	Gap	Activities / tasks	Success measure	Start Date	End Date	Actual Outcome
1. Reinforce accountability for improving incident management service-level compliance.	Staff work cross functionally to resolve incidents Teamwork is heightened and department silos are minimized Strong focus on metrics to drive improvement and understand challenge areas	IT silos impact the ability to meet service levels Staff at all levels are not held accountable for service level agreement (SLA) compliance	Create baseline metrics for existing process Develop objectives for management team and staff Conduct focus group regarding necessary process and system enhancements Communicate expectations Provide training and documentation	Compliance against service levels Progress against objectives Employee satisfaction scores	Captured in the project plan		TBD

2. Increase IT staff engagement in determining process improvement opportunities.	Staff suggest ways to be more effective in supporting the business Staff input is valued by the management team Team members are tasked with implementing suggested improvements	Staff rarely make suggestions for improvement Leaders may not acknowledge suggestions appropriately	Develop incentives plan to encourage suggestions Create a process for submitting suggestions Form a review council including cross functional leadership and staff	Increase in number of suggestions Improved employee engagement scores Percentage of suggestions implemented	Captured in the project plan	TBD

Table 1: Organizational change plan template

6: Planning

Communication plan

Communication is vital to the success of any organizational change. The communication plan outlines the communication required to achieve the desired state noted in the gap analysis. When creating the communication plan, focus not only on communication that is "pushed" to affected parties, but also on communication options which allow for individuals to "pull" information when they feel it is needed. Allowing affected parties to pull information when needed, allows them to have access in a just-in-time manner. While communication is provided throughout the project, it isn't necessarily needed by everyone until they reach a critical point in their process. In addition, the ITIL initiative probably isn't the only change occurring in the company. The amount of communication occurring can be overwhelming. Options should always be provided to access information when it is needed, in addition to being proactive and pushing communications throughout the project or initiative.

The ITIL materials provide guidance relating to creating a communication plan by outlining the purpose, frequency, audience, content, and context/sources. The communication plan example provided in this book does not reflect the ITIL materials. It is merely another option for understanding the communications required for success. Many different communication plan templates exist which will allow for appropriate planning.

When communicating about the upcoming changes, or in general about the initiative, it is important to understand the audience and their needs. One strategy is to go wide in terms of audience definition. It can be difficult to define communication needs in some organizations, so it is better

6: Planning

to be more inclusive and transparent in communications, rather than to inadvertently ignore a potential affected party, or create a sense of exclusivity.

A communication planning process can benefit the project by outlining those affected, key messages, strategies for delivering the message, and details of those accountable for communication. While the plan can stand on its own, the tasks defined can be added to the project plan for execution. A plan may already exist for the tactical changes associated with the project. In this case, the plan should be expanded to include references to, or tasks associated with, the organizational change that is necessary. In some cases, the two will overlap as early and often communication of any change to how a job is completed helps to facilitate organizational change. If a communication plan does not exist for the initiative, the steps noted can be followed for both organizational and tactical changes.

When creating the communication plan, it is wise to involve the entire project team to ensure everyone is working toward the same objective. Most likely, members of the project team will have tasks assigned to them, so it is good to involve them from the early stages.

To create the communication plan, the audience should first be defined, along with their project role, functional role, and department/company. When determining the audience, consider who is affected. Most likely, with an ITIL implementation, there will be various process owners, their supervisors or managers, functional areas such as network operations, the service desk, or the data center, customers, and other areas depending on the organization. Don't be surprised if the list is longer than originally envisioned. When defining the audience, it is very common to believe only three to four roles will be impacted, only to realize the list is much longer.

Once the audience is defined, their communication needs should be considered. For each role, ask how they will be impacted. Answering this question will allow the project to plan the required communication for each role. Do they merely need a high-level project status? Will their job be directly impacted, so they need ongoing updates, as well as detailed information regarding how to complete the processes and procedures associated with their job? Are they managing staff that are directly affected? Do they need awareness of project-related decisions and scheduling issues? By defining their communication needs, the project can ensure that they are appropriately informed and engaged as needed. When reviewing communication needs, consider the various stages of the change model.

Next, determine how to communicate with the individuals noted. Are they project participants? Is e-mail appropriate? When is a face-to-face meeting required? By understanding their communication needs, it is easier to determine the appropriate method of communication. It may be that several methods are used depending on the message that is being delivered.

Stakeholder name	Project role	Functional role / title	Organization	Information needs	Method
Robert Tucker	Program champion	CIO	IT	• Program status	• Meetings • E-mail
Jane Doe	Program sponsor	IT Vice President	IT	• High-level status regarding program • Program organization and contacts • Program-level awareness and information (budget, objectives, direction, metrics, progress, etc.)	• IT portal • E-mail • Staff meetings

Stakeholder name	Project role	Functional role / title	Organization	Information needs	Method
Gisele Rose	Engage and support the program as required	IT Manager	IT Customer Service	• Engagement in project • Program organization and contacts • Program-level awareness and information (objectives, direction, metrics, progress, etc.)	• IT portal • E-mail • Staff meetings

Table 2: Defining stakeholders and their communication needs

Based on the audience and communication required, the key messages should be outlined. They don't need to be written until time for execution, however, key points should be identified and included in the communication plan. Identify the timing of the message delivery, but also consider the preparation/review time that may be required. Based on the project plan, when should the communication occur, or when should the audience be engaged? In addition, consider if the message needs to be delivered in various languages? Will this add to the preparation time?

Assign responsibility for each communication item. If the project team members are the appropriate responsible parties, it is easier to ensure completion of the task. In some cases, it may be necessary for a senior leader to convey messages to reflect the importance of the message and the project. When asking senior leadership to communicate, it may be appropriate to draft the message, including the key points for them as a starting point. Remember, while there may be strong buy-in for the project, the senior leaders are not as engaged in the day-to-day details, and their schedules are usually challenging. Providing them with a starting point is always recommended. It also helps the project team to ensure key messages are delivered, which helps with not only the day-to-day operational changes, but also the organizational changes that are required to be successful.

Finally, include information in the communication plan relating to how success will be measured. While the project team may opt not to measure the effectiveness of every communication item, at a minimum, measurement should occur at pre-defined intervals, so adjustments can be made as needed. Gathering this information also provides details regarding how to improve results going forward, for both the ITIL initiative as well as future projects.

	1	2	3	4	5	6	7	8	9	10	11	12
Languages available												
Timing — Draft due												
Timing — Starting on	Manage as tasks in the project plan											
Timing — Frequency												
Responsibility — Delivery												
Responsibility — Preparation												
Communication method												
Key message												
Audience/ stakeholder												
Technique #	1	2	3	4	5	6	7	8	9	10	11	12
Completed												

Table 3: Project communication plan

6: Planning

Planning tips and techniques

In _Chapter 3_, five organizational change models were reviewed. Guidance regarding selecting a change model was then provided in _Chapter 4_. For each lifecycle stage and process being implemented or changed, when creating the organizational change plan, information should be gathered to determine the desired behavior changes, metrics, and mindset changes.

Each organizational change model places significant emphasis on communication and planning. When creating the organizational change plans, engage process owners and operational teams that are affected by the change. Engagement of those affected not only provides the opportunity to gather some great input, but it also enhances the process owner's understanding of why the change needs to occur and the true impact on the division, department, and individual employee. It also helps to build a solid foundation for the change plan, communications plan, and future discussions.

While planning for organizational change should start early in the project; if the ITIL process implementation represents a major change for the organization, communication about the initiative is best started at the project inception. During the creation of the organizational change plan, consideration should be given to communicating with the entire IT organization about the purpose of the project, why the project was selected and funded, the consequences of not doing this work, as well as the intended outcomes.

The organizational change and communication plans should be iterative. While work needs to occur to develop the initial plans, it is important to routinely update the plans when critical decisions are made, to ensure that the organization is on track to deliver on the desired state that was defined, as well as the general success factors and cost savings that may have been identified for the larger project.

For the initial planning and the subsequent updating of the plans, engage those affected by the changes in a focus group or interview. Discuss the positive and negative aspects of the change. Build the organizational change and communication plan tasks using the information provided. If there appears to be misunderstandings about the project purpose, or rumors about layoffs or some other misinformation, most likely it will come out in the focus groups or interviews. Address misinformation noted in communications and activities to minimize or reduce negativity which can result in organizational churn, attrition, and poor morale.

In addition to conducting focus groups with those affected by the changes, consider engaging managers and other leadership to understand what training and behavior changes are necessary for their staff to be successful in completing their day-to-day responsibilities. Ask each manager to provide a list of individuals affected by the change, specifically pointing out those that are substantially affected, as the process changed directly affects the work they do every day.

Engage those closest to the work in a discussion about the current state and discuss the potential changes necessary to meet the overall project objectives. If possible, this session should occur without leadership in the room, so the team feels comfortable having a candid conversation. A general project overview should be provided along with timelines, key milestones, an example of the metrics that may be associated with success, and the overall expected project outcomes. Discuss any key learning to date, as well as the process for selecting the project and determining the specific changes that needed to occur. Show the team the gap analysis and ask for their input about the training and documentation they need to be successful. Compiling this information and understanding the viewpoint of those affected can provide significant information for the organizational change, communication, and project plans. It also helps those individuals responsible for the outcome of the processes being implemented, or changed, to invest in the change itself.

As the implementation date associated with the project draws closer, continue having open discussions with the leaders and frontline staff that are affected by the upcoming process-related changes. Keep an open dialogue going with them, inquiring often if they have what they need to be successful when the implementation occurs. Suggest potential activities to strengthen their knowledge of the changes and increase their comfort level. While continuing these conversations during planning and implementation cycles is time consuming, it is an effective way of managing risk, reducing potential challenges, and strengthening the overall implementation. In every interaction, there is an opportunity for feedback which can improve the overall effectiveness of the project.

Several of the change models discussed include aspects which relate to solidifying the change outcomes in the organization. This task is frequently overlooked, or left to line managers, yet it is important to maintain positive momentum. While the project manager and others may be moving on to the next initiative, or system-related project, it is important that the changes implemented be reinforced.

Assess options for reinforcement during every stage of the lifecycle for every process. Long after the project is completed, reinforcement can occur through performance appraisals, monitoring metrics, and leadership.

As noted throughout this book, metrics play an important part in understanding momentum, challenge areas, and further, holding people accountable. Just as the project establishes goals, milestones, and metrics for the ITIL process implementation, when planning for organizational change, the same three areas should be evaluated. In many cases, the project-related goals, milestones, and metrics will be indicative of positive momentum occurring within the organization, however, depending on the breadth of organizational change required, consideration should be given to creating these just for organizational change. Both tangible and intangible outcomes should be considered.

How do the values of the organization need to change in order to ensure success? Does the IT team need to embrace continual service improvement? Does the ITSM office want feedback from employees on how to improve the efficiency and effectiveness of the service provided? What changes need to occur between IT and the business it supports? Answering these types of questions will help to determine potential goals, milestones, and metrics for organizational change.

Some examples of metrics associated with organizational change may include:

- improvement in response and resolution times for incidents, requests, or events
- higher IT employee engagement and satisfaction scores
- increased customer satisfaction

- increased suggestions for improving IT service
- improvement in the quality of IT changes
- a stronger sense of teamwork throughout the IT organization
- shorter implementation times for new technology.

Depending on the organization and the size and scope of the ITIL initiative, the examples noted above may or may not apply. Metrics will vary for every organization. Establish baselines for each of the metrics, in order to enable understanding of both positive and negative momentum as the project progresses. Further, reporting on the metrics throughout the life of the project will help to solidify the changes and the outcomes. Publicizing the metrics will encourage those who may not be supportive to comply with the required changes.

In addition to establishing metrics for the project, consider setting performance-related objectives for the IT staff affected by the changes. It is important to take a 360-degree view of the process and those affected. Successful implementation of the changes may require the engagement of multiple teams. Consideration should be given to establishing performance-related objectives for every individual who potentially influences the success of the initiative. Engage respective leaders in this conversation suggesting objectives as appropriate. Establish shared metrics, if possible, to encourage teamwork amongst those responsible for success.

In some organizations, discussing performance objectives relating to a project can be highly political. Some managers may view this conversation as an encroachment on their responsibilities and they may not appreciate a project manager providing suggestions in this area. If this is a true statement regarding the environment, consider establishing shared department goals for all departments affected by the ITIL process-related changes. Again, these metrics can be publicized and department-related metrics can be monitored to identify both incremental progress and challenge areas. Department-related metrics should be considered, even if individual performance objectives are established.

Throughout this book, publicizing metrics as well as success and challenge areas has been mentioned. To facilitate change and encourage an environment of trust, when publicizing this information, the message should center on making improvements to the service that is ultimately delivered to the customer. When communication is done in the spirit of improvement, ideas for change will come from the IT team. In addition, creating a safe environment for trying out new ideas, and making it acceptable to fail, will facilitate out-of-the-box thinking and improved collaboration on future projects and improvement initiatives.

Finally, when implementing the ITIL process-related changes, consider engaging the business. If significant changes are occurring in the IT organization, it is important to set expectations with them. As they are the customer, they will often see improvements before the metrics show the results. They will also quickly experience difficulty if there are process-related challenges, or underlying organizational issues. It is beneficial to conduct interviews or focus groups with the business when planning the overall ITIL-related initiative. They will provide insight into their needs, as well as their view of organizational change-related challenges. At the very least, discussions should occur with the business about the changes IT is hoping to achieve. Engaging the business in these conversations will demonstrate that IT understands that they exist to support the business in achieving their outcomes in an efficient and effective manner. It will show a spirit of partnership.

CHAPTER 7: IMPORTANT ROLES

Now that you have a solid start on the change plan, it is time to consider the implementation. Whether you are ready to actually begin the implementation, or you have inserted a placeholder in the project plan for organizational change-related activities, additional planning is necessary to ensure success.

Roles and responsibilities

An important aspect of organizational change entails determining the owner of the organizational change activities. Within almost every stage of the implementation, there are change activities occurring. Who is ultimately responsible for ensuring those tasks occur? Perhaps it is the project manager who is driving the project and ensuring tasks are complete. It is great to have someone manage the project, but, ultimately, the project sponsor is accountable. Every key stakeholder also owns a portion of this work. With organizational change, communication is key and communication showing support for the change from leadership is imperative. In addition, managers who are leading staff that will be affected by the change are key players to ensuring success. Project participants should also be assigned organizational-related change tasks. When assigning tasks associated with organizational change, consider the skill sets of the individual. Chapter 9 includes a list of the top 10 skills for change agents (*see Table 4*).

Engage as many stakeholders, leaders, and project participants as possible to participate in organizational change. During the planning process, outline all of the tasks based on the change and also who will be impacted. Keep in mind that the business may recognize an impact from the implementation, so engage the right business stakeholder(s) to ensure they are aware and prepared to effectively support the initiative.

Also, consider if there is one person within the organization that could effectively manage the role of **Change Evangelist**. A change evangelist is an enthusiastic, charismatic, well-respected advocate of the change being implemented. Within most organizations, there is someone with "professional presence"; they project confidence, ability, and integrity. They communicate well and they are well respected. This person is a good choice for the role of change evangelist. In this role, they would take every opportunity to promote what is occurring. This role would often bring up the benefits of what is occurring and tie the initiative to other changes within the company. Often, the role of change evangelist requires little additional work, as the assigned individual merely changes how they deliver messages in their daily work and they attend a small number of additional meetings. They can become a powerful ally for the project team.

In addition to the change evangelist, there are some key roles within any change initiative.

The **Change Agent** is often responsible for coordinating the overall change effort. In most ITSM initiatives, the project manager fills this role, however, in larger organizations, someone may be assigned to coordinate all organizational change activities, as the sheer size of an organization may require a dedicated team member. It is common for the role of change agent to transition during the life of a project based on circumstances.

The **Change Champion** is similar to the evangelist role. Sometimes, the evangelist and the champion are one and the same. The champion's role is to continuously communicate and explain why the IT Infrastructure Library process initiative is taking place and the expected benefits.

Finally, the **Change Sponsor** is the executive who is sponsoring the IT Infrastructure Library (ITIL) project. They are ultimately responsible for success of the project and, therefore, the importance of the organizational aspect of the change is understood. The sponsor often assists with organizational change by providing high-level communications to those affected, showing support for the initiative, allocating resources, and seeking support from Human Resources for the project (if necessary).

Build the organizational change-related tasks into the project plan with dates and resources assigned. Consider engaging the corporate communications team, or, if you are unable to seek internal professional assistance, identify someone on the team whose strength is written communication. To ensure the right messages are communicated, the communications resource should draft key talking points for leaders to use when communicating about the project. Consider the roles of the change evangelist, change agent, change champion, and change sponsor when assigning organizational change tasks.

Governance

Projects usually include governance and a reporting structure of some sort. If the implementation is not considered a project, someone at a high level is overseeing the process-related implementation and for purposes of this section, this oversight should be considered the governing body. Rarely do governing bodies manage organizational change, yet their help is needed to maximize the chances of success. Organizational change plans are most likely new to the company, so adding a layer of governance is a positive step toward reinforcing the importance. The same governance structure currently in place for a larger ITIL initiative can be used for managing organizational change, as success of the project is directly linked to the organization's behavior.

ITIL guidance notes that an IT Strategy and Steering Committee is the IT governance body. If the organization has this governing body, it is appropriate to discuss organizational change planning, progress, resources requirements, and issues with this group. This Committee is charged with meeting regularly to review business and IT governance, as well as strategies, culture, policies, designs, plans, portfolios, architectures, and processes. Note that culture is part of their mission.

If a governance structure will not work within the organization, consider a subset of the project team, ITIL process owners, or perhaps some key operational leaders, or those with the change-related roles noted earlier in this chapter, as the organizational change committee. The purpose of the committee, or governing structure, is to assist with the following aspects of the organizational change:

- Understand the critical aspect of the changes required, so they can speak to them when necessary, emphasizing the positive aspects and outcomes expected.

- Provide guidance relating to organizational change-related risks and challenges.
- Provide access to the resources (staff, funding, etc.) required for success.
- Discuss opportunities to leverage communications, training activities, events, influencing behavior, etc. across departments.
- Review performance against key performance indicators, as well as other metrics associated with the organizational change activities outlined for the project.
- Obtain ongoing executive and leadership support for the changes required for success of the project and long-term sustainment of the changes within the organization.

The overarching goal of any IT governance body is to ensure that IT is effectively aligned with the business and delivering value. Addressing organizational change as a component of the overall ITIL process-related initiative is imperative to maximizing the opportunity for success and, therefore, the IT governance body should welcome discussions relating to risks and challenge areas, as well as progress reports solidified by metrics.

CHAPTER 8: REALIZING THE BENEFITS AFTER THE FACT

Every IT organization has some aspects of ITIL long before they embark on a journey to improve their processes, or to conduct a formal implementation. ITIL is merely a structured, documented set of best practices. Most organizations have some way of responding to incidents and requests, and, usually, even if the organization did not undertake any type of ITIL-related initiative, there is some commonality in how they handle an incident or a request and the ITIL best practices.

Naturally, organizations often set out to improve processes, yet, at times, processes seem to get worse, or a change does not occur. Why aren't the intended improvements realized? There are a number of reasons why this could occur. The intended outcome may not have been possible given existing constraints, such as technology or staffing. At times though, the organizational change required may have become the barrier restricting the organization from realizing the benefits.

Once the change is implemented, how can the organization realize the change that was originally desired – after the fact? It can be done; however, additional work is required.

One of the first steps towards improving the existing state is to measure what is currently taking place. What did the process initiative intend to improve? What was the intended outcome? Without truly understanding the current state, it will be difficult to know when the desired outcome is reached. If metrics existed prior to the process improvement, they should also be gathered. This allows for an understanding of the impact of the changes.

Once the current state is known, the desired state may require definition. What is the intended outcome of the changes being implemented? Critical success factors should be understood. What are the crucial elements of the process being implemented? The crucial or essential elements are often considered critical success factors.

The metrics about the current state should support the critical success factors. These metrics are also known as key performance indicators. Based on the critical success factors and the metrics regarding the current state, a review should be conducted to determine if additional metrics are required.

With any initiative resulting in a change to how people work, engaging those affected is always important to solidify buy-in, but also to uncover elements that may be unknown to those who do not perform the task. If the ITIL process implementation did not create the desired end state that was expected, the true cause may not be known. Engage those directly impacted by the changes to understand why the end state was not realized.

Observation is one method of improving the understanding of why the changes were not realized. Who is responsible for completing the task? Shadowing these individuals will enable an understanding of what is occurring today and why. It is important when observing the process not to criticize or pass judgment on what is occurring. The goal is merely to collect information as to what is happening. Often, barriers to success are uncovered that were unknown at the time of the implementation.

Focus groups are another great method for obtaining feedback regarding trouble spots. Gathering a group of individuals affected by the change and asking pointed questions will often result in great feedback regarding challenges with the existing process, and potential solutions. When conducting a focus group, it is important to keep the tone of the conversation unbiased and to ensure everyone understands that the purpose is process improvement. One great method of avoiding too much negativity is to ask a question and ask the participants to write their answers on a piece of paper. They then hand the paper to the facilitator who reads the answers and gathers additional input from the team. One component of the input is for the group to provide options for improvement.

Now that those affected have provided feedback, observation of the existing process has occurred, and there is an understanding of the current state, consideration of the necessary changes to achieve the desired end result can take place. Have the goals of the initiative changed? Solidify the goals associated with the change. Why is this change taking place?

Once the goals and metrics are understood, planning for the initiative should once again take place. As outlined in *Chapter 6*, a project plan, organizational change plan, and communication plan should be drafted. Despite recognizing that this may not be a formal project, as the initial implementation is being revisited, planning still needs to occur. Most, if not all, of the planning elements noted throughout this book still apply.

Rather than governance or a formal project team, an improvement committee may be formed recognizing that the intended changes associated with the original process initiative did not occur and the root cause of the issue must be addressed. The committee would address the root cause and prepare a course of action. Again, a plan which includes organizational change and communication aspects should be prepared and roles and responsibilities assigned.

The use of one of the change models discussed in *Chapter 3* can help to provide some guidance with addressing the organizational changes that may be required for success. For example, the ADKAR change model can be used to ensure that those affected have the tools, knowledge, and motivation to be successful when adopting the change. Awareness, Desire, Knowledge, Ability, and Reinforcement tasks would be included in the plan to readdress the IT Infrastructure Library process initiative.

When evaluating why the initial change was unsuccessful through using metrics, focus groups, and/or observation, it is most likely that some resistance to change will be uncovered. It is critical that the resistance also be addressed. Consider using the core techniques of the Six Change, or one of the other organizational change models noted in *Chapter 3* when planning to manage resistance to the change. Reviewing these techniques with the leadership of those directly impacted by the change, and sharing any observations about individuals, would be a significant step toward addressing resistance. If available, metrics regarding individual performance relating to this change could also be shared, and routine measurements considered as part of ongoing sustainment activities.

CHAPTER 9: ADDITIONAL GUIDANCE

Throughout this book, engagement of resources across the organization is stressed. Motivation occurs in varying ways and it is based on the individual, so it is important to engage staff at varying levels in the change process. When assigning organizational change-related tasks to individuals in the organization, it is important to consider their level of skill in critical areas. Change facilitation is not an easy task. Certain skills are crucial to success as change affects people in different ways and a change facilitator will encounter varying types of resistance.

Critical skills

The following table (*Table 4: Top 10 skills for change agents*) notes 10 critical skills for anyone filling a change-related role. While every position will require a unique set of experiences, skills, and abilities, change-related roles, such as those mentioned in *Chapter 7*, are challenging and the skills noted overleaf are the basic skills required for success. Additional skills may be required based on the culture within an organization.

When filling the role of change agent, change evangelist, change sponsor, and change champion, consider if the individuals have strong skills, as noted overleaf.

9: Additional Guidance

Skill	Explained
Active listening	Being present in the moment, completely focused on what is being said, and then re-stating the information or paraphrasing the information to ensure understanding.
Interviewing and questioning	Solicits input and feedback by asking for pertinent information often transitioning topics, or referencing earlier discussion naturally, based on a word or comment made during the course of the discussion.
Non-verbal communication	Understands the messages that are sent through body language, gestures, eye contact, and facial expressions; appropriately solicits additional information based on these cues.
Verbal communication	Verbally engages others with analogies and stories that relate to the topic, thereby translating complex information, so it is easy to understand.
Written communication	Through the use of words, formatting, and diagrams, communicates important and sometimes complex information in a written format.
Negotiation	Able to exchange information with the intent of reaching an understanding, agreement, or acceptable outcome.
Building trust	Through open communication, integrity, honesty, and ability, develops faith in intention and outcomes.

Tenacity	Seeks to overcome obstacles by examining potential solutions, and seeking assistance and guidance as necessary, to achieve the desired result.
Time management	Plans for projects and tasks to ensure maximum productivity and completion of work within the required timeframe.
Persuasion	Ability to influence motivations, beliefs, behaviors, attitudes, and intentions through logic, reasoning, and relating key points to real world or meaningful situations

Table 4: Top 10 skills for change agents

When determining who will fill important change-related roles, it is important to gain senior leadership support and participation. To minimize potential resistance, engage staff that are not part of the process improvement team, if appropriate. Staff in operational roles can significantly influence others in similar roles. Operational staff tend to have similar day-to-day responsibilities. If an operational staff member fills a change-related role, it may be easier for others in similar roles to support the changes, as their colleagues are visibly engaged and supportive.

Four areas for success

The implementation of an ITIL initiative is complex, however, throughout this book, there are four themes present within all of the discussions and activities taking place. If focus is placed in these four areas, improvement will occur. The depth and breadth of the focus will determine how much improvement is realized.

9: Additional Guidance

1. Planning for organizational change

While new processes, services, and systems can be implemented without any difficulty at all, true organizational change may or may not have occurred. Acceptance may only be surface level with a fair amount of time wasted by employees talking about the challenges, or disagreeing with the changes.

Organizational change should be planned. When planned as part of a project, the end result will be of a higher caliber. While it may not be a perfect implementation, the risk will be lower as staff have been engaged; efficiency will be higher as there will be a focus on making improvements when things go wrong, rather than complaining; service to the customer will remain at a constant level, if not improve, as staff are prepared to do the work; and relationships will be enhanced, as staff are working together as a team to achieve the appropriate result.

2. Communicate about the project. Do it early. Do it often. Do it well.

Employees talk and rumors spread, however, what is actually occurring with a project is most likely only known by those closest to the action on a daily basis. A full-blown ITIL project can have a substantial impact on an IT organization. If IT staff have attended ITIL training, they've probably heard about reorganizations or positions changing.

To build support and momentum for the ITIL initiative, communicate with the entire organization about the project right from the start. After the initial communication, which describes the "who, what, why, where, how, and when" of the ITIL project, communications should be targeted to the appropriate group, but occur frequently with broader communication going out as needed.

It is important that all levels of leadership are engaged and appropriately prepared for questions. In addition, employees should have a way of reaching out to project-related resources for information.

Division meetings, staff meetings, e-mail, newsletters, intranets, lunch and learn sessions, screensavers, and information tables in the cafeteria are all potential avenues for communication. Use the communication mechanism that makes sense for the organization, but communicate frequently and be as open and straightforward as possible.

3. Engage the staff in the project

The IT team is comprised of many talented individuals. Even in the most dysfunctional organizations, there are talented people who are merely reacting to the circumstance of their surroundings. The IT staff are doing the jobs that are affected by the ITIL project. They are the closest to the actual work.

For better results with fewer issues, engage those closest to the work that is changing. They will provide valuable insight and history that should be considered when changing the strategy, principles, or processes.

Involving the affected staff, teams, and leadership will also build support and buy-in for the change. It reduces fear, uncertainty, and doubt. It allows for better planning and communication.

Focus groups, interviews, project meetings, surveys, observation, brainstorming, system demonstrations, and requirements sessions are all examples of opportunities to engage staff in the project. Every company has its own cultural norm which provides unique opportunities for involvement. Use every opportunity available to talk with the people affected.

4. Measure the current state, set goals, routinely measure progress, and publicize the outcomes.

Without metrics, how is success defined? How does one understand the current state and truly understand the impact of a change?

Even if the ITIL initiative involves improving one process, rather than a full-blown implementation, the current state metrics should be defined and performance understood. In some organizations, metrics do not exist, as there are data-related challenges. These types of challenges exist in every organization. The difference is that some look for meaningful metrics and work to find a way to understand the current state, rather than merely indicating it can't be done.

The power of metrics can generate positive change. Publicizing the improvements and challenge areas using metrics can have a dramatic result. When the right goals are set and accountability is in place, metrics can: tear down silos by highlighting teams that may be having challenges; find unexpected opportunities where changes may not be having the intended results; provide focus to financial savings, as well as investment opportunities for the IT budget; build camaraderie, as success can be celebrated;

and identify new services required to meet business outcomes.

Metrics relating to the ITIL project and, further, related ongoing operations should be a focus area from project inception through implementation and beyond. For the staff, transparency regarding IT performance through the use of established metrics will build support and understanding within the IT team.

Organizational change is not easy. It can and does happen organically, however, if organizations wait for it to happen without planning, the result may not be what is required and it will take an immense amount of time.

Addressing organizational change as part of the ITIL initiative, or, really, as part of any project, will help to minimize potential issues, improve employee engagement and morale, increase the velocity of change, achieve stronger results, and build stronger teams.

The five change models discussed in this book all have their benefits. They were selected due to their unique nature. Every organization should choose the model(s) right for them. As with any framework, the planning and execution will play a significant role in success. To reiterate, every organization will experience some positive momentum by concentrating on the four focus areas noted above: planning, communication, engagement, and metrics. The amount of improvement will be based on the depth and breadth of time spent in each of these areas.

The IT Infrastructure Library is a powerful framework to help to build the IT Service Management approach, but process, by itself, will not accomplish the result. The people in the organization and their commitment to the changes and the overall vision and mission will, ultimately, determine success. To achieve support for the project and maximize the opportunity for success, it is imperative to address organizational change.

REFERENCES

Boyatzis, R., McKee, A. & Goleman, D. (2004) *Primal Leadership: Learning to Lead with Emotional Intelligence*, Harvard Business Review Press.

Goleman, D. (2005) *Emotional Intelligence: Why It Can Matter More Than IQ*, Bantam Books; 10th Anniversary Edition.

Harter, J. K., Schmidt, F.L. and Keyes, C.L.M. (2003) Well-being in the workplace and its relationship to business outcomes: A review of the Gallup studies. In C.L.M. Keyes and J Haidt (Eds) *Flourishing, Positive Psychology and the Life Well-lived*. Washington DC, USA: American Psychological Society.

Hiatt, J. M. (2006) *ADKAR: A Model for Change in Business, Government, and our Community*. Prosci Learning Center Publications, 1st Edition.

Kotter, J. P. and Schleisinger, L.A. (1979) Choosing Strategies for Change, *Harvard Business Review*, Mar-Apr.

Kotter, J.P. (1996) *Leading Change*, Harvard Business School Press.

Lewin, K. (1947) *Frontiers in Group Dynamics*, Bobbs-Merrill, College Division.

Pascale, R. (1991) *Managing on the Edge*, Penguin Books.

Peters, T. & Waterman, R. (1984) *In Search of Excellence*, Recorded Books, Inc.

References

Rance, S. (2011) *ITIL Service Transition 2011 Edition*, The Stationery Office.

APPENDIX 1: ITIL CONSULTING AND ADVANCED ORGANIZATIONAL PERFORMANCE TECHNIQUES ™

Advanced Organizational Performance Techniques, also known as AdOPT™, developed by Pamela Erskine, focuses on organizational change to ensure success with your ITIL initiative. If your organization is undertaking an ITIL project, Pamela's team can help by providing guidance and techniques based on best practices. Listed below are examples of the wide range of consulting services offered.

Advanced Organizational Performance Techniques (AdOPT) consulting services:

- Organizational Change Vision and Strategy Workshops
- Cultural assessments to identify the ideal change model
- Development of organizational change plans and metrics
- Consulting to identify organizational change tasks and opportunities
- Critical Change Skills training for Leaders
- Coaching and mentoring for organizational change.

ITIL consulting services:

- ITIL and Project Vision and Strategy Definition
- Process assessments and design
- Service Catalog definition

Appendix 1: ITIL Consulting and Advanced Organizational Performance Techniques ™

- Identification of IT services
- Department/Team assessments
- ITIL coaching and mentoring.

For more information, visit *www.adoptitil.com*

ITG RESOURCES

IT Governance Ltd. sources, creates and delivers products and services to meet the real-world, evolving IT governance needs of today's organizations, directors, managers and practitioners.

The ITG website (*www.itgovernance.co.uk*) is the international one-stop-shop for corporate and IT governance information, advice, guidance, books, tools, training, and consultancy.

Other Websites

Books and tools published by IT Governance Publishing (ITGP) are available from all business booksellers and are also immediately available from the following websites:

www.itgovernance.eu is our euro-denominated website which ships from Benelux and has a growing range of books in European languages other than English.

www.itgovernanceusa.com is a US$-based website that delivers the full range of IT Governance products to North America, and ships from within the continental US.

www.itgovernanceasia.com provides a selected range of ITGP products specifically for customers in the Indian sub-continent.

www.itgovernance.asia delivers the full range of ITGP publications, serving countries across Asia Pacific. Shipping from Hong Kong, US dollars, Singapore dollars, Hong Kong dollars, New Zealand dollars and Thai baht are all accepted through the website.

Toolkits

ITG's unique range of toolkits includes the IT Governance Framework Toolkit, which contains all the tools and guidance that you will need in order to develop and implement an appropriate IT governance framework for your organisation. For a free paper on how to use the proprietary Calder-Moir IT Governance Framework, and for a free trial version of the toolkit, see *www.itgovernance.co.uk/calder_moir.aspx*.

There is also a wide range of toolkits to simplify implementation of management systems, such as an ISO/IEC 27001 ISMS or an ISO/IEC 22301 BCMS, and these can all be viewed and purchased online at *www.itgovernance.co.uk*.

Training Services

IT Governance offer an extensive portfolio of training courses designed to educate information security, IT governance, risk management, and compliance professionals. Our classroom and online training programs will help you develop the skills required to deliver best practice and compliance to your organization. They will also enhance your career by providing you with industry standard certifications and increased peer recognition. Our range of courses offer a structured learning path from Foundation to Advanced level in the key topics of information security, IT governance, business continuity, and service management.

ISO/IEC 20000 is the first international standard for IT service management and has been developed to reflect the best practice guidance contained within the ITIL framework. Our ISO20000 Foundation and Practitioner training courses are designed to provide delegates with a comprehensive introduction and guide to the implementation of an ISO20000 management system and an industry recognised qualification awarded by APMG International.

Full details of all IT Governance training courses can be found at *www.itgovernance.co.uk/training.aspx*.

Professional Services and Consultancy

If you are reading this book, you are probably working on an ITIL project that involves organizational change management. Support from our expert consultants can be transformational in terms of improving IT services and, ultimately, the business – and there is no time like the present to put our team to the test.

It is common for organizations to apply ITIL best practices and yet never realise the full benefits of that implementation. Our consultants can empower you to achieve organizational change, including behaviours, attitudes, and culture, through the introduction of effective change management processes.

Our experts can also coach and mentor in the requirements of the emerging international standard for IT service management. ISO20000 will enable your organization to adopt an integrated process approach to improved IT service management; one in which you plan, establish, implement, operate, monitor, review, maintain, and improve a service management system (SMS).

For more information about IT Governance Consultancy services, see *www.itgovernance.co.uk/itsm-itil-iso20000-consultancy.aspx*.

Publishing Services

IT Governance Publishing (ITGP) is the world's leading IT-GRC publishing imprint that is wholly owned by IT Governance Ltd.

With books and tools covering all IT governance, risk, and compliance frameworks, we are the publisher of choice for authors and distributors alike, producing unique and practical publications of the highest quality, in the latest formats available, which readers will find invaluable.

www.itgovernancepublishing.co.uk is the website dedicated to ITGP enabling both current and future authors, distributors, readers, and other interested parties, to have easier access to more information. This allows ITGP website visitors to keep up to date with the latest publications and news.

Newsletter

IT governance is one of the hottest topics in business today, not least because it is also the fastest moving.

You can stay up to date with the latest developments across the whole spectrum of IT governance subject matter, including: risk management, information security, ITIL® and IT service management, project governance, compliance, and so much more, by subscribing to ITG's core publications and topic alert e-mails.

Simply visit our subscription center and select your preferences: *www.itgovernance.co.uk/newsletter.aspx*